# A LAYMAN'S GUIDE TO Studying THE BIBLE

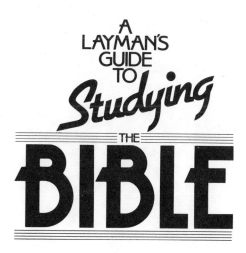

# A LAYMAN'S GUIDE TO
# *Studying*
# THE
# BIBLE

## Walter Henrichsen

**Lamplighter Books** Grand Rapids, Michigan
Zondervan Publishing House

A Layman's Guide to Studying the Bible

This is a Lamplighter Book
Published by the Zondervan Publishing House
1415 Lake Drive, S.E., Grand Rapids, Michigan 49506

**Library of Congress Cataloging in Publication Data**

Henrichsen, Walter A.
   A layman's guide to studying the Bible.

   "Lamplighter books."
   1. Bible—Study.   2. Bible—Text-books.   I. Title.
BS605.2.H46   1985      220'.07      85-26387
ISBN 0-310-37631-9

*Printed in the United States of America*

86  87  88  89  90  91  92  93  /  10  9  8  7  6  5  4  3  2  1

# Contents

# SECTION

# I

# How to Study the Bible

# 1
## Bible Study Is for Everyone

The scene before our eyes is the vast expanse of wilderness between Jerusalem and the Jordan River. In preparation for His public ministry, Jesus had fasted 40 days and nights in this barren expanse, alone, hungry, and weary. Satan now confronts Him with three insidious temptations. Three times our Lord wards off his suggestions by quoting from the Book of Deuteronomy.

Recognizing that the Bible is authoritative for the Savior, Satan tries his hand at quoting Scripture too. He selects the psalmist's statement, "For he will command his angels concerning you to guard you in all your ways; they will lift you up in their hands, so that you will not strike your foot against a stone" (Psalm 91:11-12; see Matthew 4:6).

As you compare Satan's words with the text in Psalm 91, it is interesting to note that he does not *misquote* the psalmist. Rather, he misuses the passage by misrepresenting the intent of the writer.

The tactics of our enemy have not changed through the centuries. Since Satan misrepresented the Scriptures to Jesus Christ, the believer today can be assured of the same thing happening to him. But how does the devil do this? From what quarter are we to expect his attacks?

## Ways in Which the Bible May Be Misused

Five ways immediately come to mind, and others could be added to this illustrative list.

1. *The Scriptures may be misused when you are ignorant about what the Bible says on a given subject.*

The ordination of avowed, practicing homosexuals into the gospel ministry is an example. Some would have the church believe that the loving, accepting spirit of our Lord Jesus precludes their being barred from ordination. Nowhere did Jesus say they shouldn't be ordained, so the church should ordain them as clergy in good and regular standing. Yet the Old Testament expressly forbids acts of homosexuality (see Leviticus 18:22), and Paul states that homosexual behavior contributes to God's wrath on mankind (see Romans 1:26-27). Ignorance about what the Bible teaches is an open door to the attack of the enemy.

2. *The Scriptures may be misused when you take a verse out of context.*

On the night of His betrayal Jesus said to His disciples, "Until now you have not asked for anything in my name. Ask and you will receive, and your joy will be complete" (John 16:24). Some have taken this to be a carte blanche promise from God. He will grant whatever you ask. That same night, however, a short while after making this statement, Jesus prayed in the Garden of Gethsemane, "Take this cup from me. Yet not what I will, but what you will" (Mark 14:36). Promises in the Bible must be blended with the total context of the scriptural teaching on prayer (see 1 John 5:14-15).

3. *The Scriptures may be misused when you read into a passage and have it say what it doesn't say.*

Toward the end of His ministry, Jesus said, "And these signs will accompany those who believe: In my name they will drive out demons; they will speak in new tongues; they will pick up snakes with their hands; and when they drink deadly poison, it will not hurt them at all" (Mark 16:17-18). Some have taken this descriptive passage to be a command to do all of the things mentioned, reading into it a mandate to do all of these when all Jesus is doing is describing what is going to happen in situations in the early church when certain people had the gift of miracles.

4. *The Scriptures may be misused when you give undue emphasis to less important things.*

Did Judas, the betrayer of our Lord, participate with Jesus and the other disciples in the Last Supper? The evidence is inconclusive, yet some allow themselves to become greatly exercised over an issue such as this, even to the point of contributing toward disunity in the church.

5. *The Scriptures may be misused **whenever** you use the Bible to try to get God to do what you want, **rather than** what God wants done.*

Let us use the example of a woman who is in love with a man and wants very much to marry him. Jesus said, "Again, I tell you that if two of you on earth agree about anything you ask for, it will be done for you by my Father in heaven" (Matthew 18:19). Taking this promise to a girlfriend, she asks the woman to join her in claiming this promise in order to "get" the man. This is an obvious misuse of the Scriptures.

## The Need for Bible Study Methods

Not every misuse of the Bible can be attributed to an attack from Satan, even in the illustrations just mentioned. It becomes immediately apparent, however, that you must learn to use the Scriptures carefully. Christians must not only become familiar with the rules of interpretation, but they must apply these rules to a life-long habit of Bible study. The objective of this section of the book is to introduce you to Bible study methods. Much good material is already available on this subject, but the intent here is to take some methods of Bible study and make them simple enough for the average layman to incorporate into his Christian life.

Unlike the subject of interpretation, Bible study methods have a great deal of flexibility and require some creativity. These methods are not "rules" of Bible study per se, but are guidelines which, if followed, will enhance the study of the Scriptures. We will explore these methods in the following chapters. No matter how masterful or conscientious a student of the Bible you may be, you must maintain vigilance in staying fresh and creative. So experiment with the various methods. Pick and choose from what is offered and add your own ideas. Make the method yours. Remember, there is a difference between doing Bible study which can be drab and perfunctory on the one hand, and studying the Bible which is exciting and life-changing on the other.

## Principles of Bible Study

When I was a fledgling seminarian, a layman sat down with me and introduced me to five principles of Bible study. He helped me realize the importance of going to the Scriptures as my primary source, rather than gleaning spiritual truths from studies other men have made. By principles, he meant that they ought to be included in our Bible study, irrespective of the method we might employ.

1. *You must do original investigation.* An incident in the early church illustrates the importance of the believer getting alone with an open Bible and depending on the Holy Spirit to be his teacher: "Now the Bereans were of more noble character than the Thessalonians, for they received the message with great eagerness and examined the Scriptures every day to see if what Paul said was

true'' (Acts 17:11). The Bereans listened attentively to what Paul and Silas had to say, but elected to check it out with the original source.

It is important that conviction be formed on what the Bible teaches, rather than depending on creeds, commentaries, or even sermons. The latter may cause you to turn to the Word as did the Bereans, but during times of testing it is the authority of the infallible Word personally examined that stands.

Two types of resource materials may be used in Bible study. Biblical encylopedias, dictionaries, and concordances are one type, and should be the constant companion of the student. Commentaries and other expository works are the second type. But these should only be used *after* the principle of original investigation has been applied.

Referring to a good commentary after the study is completed is helpful, particularly if you teach your material to others or lead a Bible study group. It becomes a way of checking your ideas and conclusions with others. If you find yourself in disagreement with the commentator, especially on significant issues, you should then take a fresh look at *your* conclusions.

Original investigation is a necessary and important principle to incorporate into your methodology. There is something fresh and exciting about a truth taught by the Holy Spirit during your personal time in the Word of God.

2. *You must have written reproduction.* Have you ever had the experience of thinking a profound thought, but because you did not write it down you forgot it? If so, you probably discerned that the harder you tried to remember the thought, the more elusive it became. Such a frustrating experience illustrates the importance of incorporating written reproduction into your Bible study methods.

Dawson Trotman, founder of The Navigators, often would say, ''Thoughts disentangle themselves as they pass from the mind through the lips and over the finger tips.'' Writing down your thoughts and drawing them together is one of the key differences between Bible reading and Bible study. A rich reservoir of scriptural knowledge can be stored for future use when written reproduction is employed.

3. *Your study must be consistent and systematic.* Two concepts make up this third principle. Bible study should be consistent. This is implied in the words *every day* in Acts 17:11. The Bereans didn't study the Scriptures one day, then wait a week to do it again. Their approach was *consistent.*

The other concept embedded in this principle is that Bible study must be systematic. A chapter here, a topic there, a passage another time are not the best approaches to studying the Bible. Map out a program of Bible study that will systematically unfold for you a balanced understanding of God's whole Word. Such an approach is suggested in the Appendix.

4. *Your study must be ''pass-on-able.''* This conglomerate may sound strange, but it does communicate an important concept. It is found in Paul's statement to Timothy: ''And the things you have heard me say in the presence of many witnesses entrust to reliable men who will also be qualified to teach others'' (2 Timothy 2:2). It is God's intention that we not only grow and mature in our walk with Him, but also help others to maximize their potential for Jesus Christ.

Each believer is to view himself as a link between two generations. We are to *pass on* to others what we have had the privilege of learning. If we apply this only to the content of our study we encourage people to become dependent on us for ''intake.'' The biblical concept of the priesthood of the believer means that all Christians have both the right and the responsibility of feeding personally on the Word of God. Our Bible study methodology must include the element of pass-on-able-ness to facilitate this great ideal.

5. *You must apply what you study to your life.* So important is this principle that we find it incorporated in the rules of interpretation as well as the methodology about to be studied. A cursory reading of almost any portion of the Bible reveals how important application is from God's perspective. He *expects* His Word to be taken seriously. James tersely said, "Do not merely listen to the Word, and so deceive yourselves. Do what it says" (James 1:22).

## Basic Steps of Bible Study

Four essentials form the foundation for all Bible study—observation, interpretation, correlation, application. Because these parts *are* basic to your study of the Word, irrespective of the kind of study in which you engage (such as, analytical, synthetic, or topical), it is necessary to look at each individually and at some length.

Each of the four parts will be presented in such a way as to move from the simple to the more advanced. As you apply these parts to your study of the Scriptures, you will be encouraged to select your own level of difficulty, adding various techniques as you become increasingly proficient.

The format of the following chapters will introduce you to five methods of Bible study, beginning with a basic study and moving toward more advanced steps. Each of them will use the four parts of Bible study—observation, interpretation, correlation, application.

As you begin to do these studies, follow the *Basic* sections only

(to the **STOP** sign). Do *not* go on to the *Advanced* sections till

you have mastered the basic approach. The methods do not have to be done in the presented order; you may try your hand on them in any order. The basic studies on the following pages are:

After you are comfortable with any of the *Basic* approaches, you have the choice of going in two directions: (1) Proceed to do the *Advanced* steps of the method you have chosen, or (2) go more in depth in your *Basic* study by turning to the suggestions in Chapters 8–11.

If you are just beginning a program of Bible study, you may want to consider starting with a question-and-answer method to get the "feel" of it. An outstanding series on this method is *Studies in Christian Living,* published by The Navigators. (This set and individual booklets are available from your local Christian bookstore or from Customer Services, NavPress, P.O. Box 20, Colorado Springs, Colorado 80901.) This series consists of nine booklets, progressing from the simple to the more difficult. Not only do they introduce you to two Bible study methods, they also expose you to all the major teachings of the Bible.

Doing these is not a prerequisite to the material in Chapters 2–6, but if you find the following difficult, you may want to start with the question-and-answer approach.

# 2 The Verse Analysis Method of Bible Study

---

**VERSE ANALYSIS**

---

**The study of a single verse in the Bible with reference to its immediate context.**

The verse analysis method of Bible study is the simplest "on-your-own" study. But don't let its simplicity fool you. It is an extremely profitable and rewarding method of Bible study, and a wonderful place to begin. Many have found the fruits of such a study so rewarding that they find themselves continually returning to it for the feeding of their souls.

Bible study is only one method of scriptural intake. You should also be engaged in a Bible reading program. Ideally, it is from this reading program that you select the verse to be studied. In the margin of your Bible, or on a separate sheet of paper if you prefer, note possible verses to be studied.

When you are ready to begin your study, select from these possibilities the one on which you want to concentrate.

You may also want to consider the possibility of memorizing the verse. This combination of Bible study and Scripture memory is unbeatable in sealing the verse to your own heart.

To draw attention to the four basic parts of Bible study, you will note next to each step a letter indicating the part you are doing.

- **(O)** OBSERVATION
- **(I)** INTERPRETATION
- **(C)** CORRELATION
- **(A)** APPLICATION

As you become more proficient in your use of the *Verse Analysis* method, you may want to refer to the chapters dealing with these parts for additional things to look for.

## Basic Verse Analysis

For the purpose of illustration, 1 Thessalonians 5:17 will be used in walking through this procedure: "Pray without ceasing" (KJV).

**(O)** *Step One*—Select the context of the verse and note the boundaries. If it is difficult to determine this, refer to a modern translation such as the *New International Version,* which notes the paragraph divisions. If the context is a rather long paragraph, you may either want to try breaking it down further or choose another verse to study.

The context of 1 Thessalonians 5:17 is the verses immediately preceding and following: "Rejoice evermore" (verse 16 KJV) and "In everything give thanks, for this is the will of God in Christ Jesus concerning you" (verse 18 KJV).

**(O)** *Step Two*—Note any observations and/or possible applications. Also look for any problems, stating specifically what the problem is. You will want to add to this section of your study constantly as you proceed through the other steps.

## 1 THESSALONIANS 5:16-18

**(O)** • There are three commands—*rejoice, pray, give thanks.*

**(O)** • These commands all have modifiers—*evermore, without ceasing, in everything.*

**(O)** • The clause "This is the will of God in Christ Jesus concerning you" seems to apply to all three verses.

**(O)** • You can interchange the modifiers with one another without changing the meaning of the verses: *"Rejoice evermore, pray evermore, give thanks evermore,"* and so on with the other modifiers.

**(A)** • Giving thanks (verse 18) is not one of my strong points. I tend to grumble about everything.

**(A)** • I rejoice (sometimes), but not "always."

**(I)** • The modifiers all have the idea of being perpetual, that is, there is never a time when they shouldn't be done.

**(I)** • Can verse 17 be taken literally? Is it possible to pray unceasingly? Or is Paul simply talking about an attitude here?

**(I)** *Step Three*—Briefly rewrite each of the verses in your own words. Try to express the kernel of thought or main idea the writer is communicating.

## 1 THESSALONIANS 5:16-18

• Verse 16—Never stop rejoicing
• Verse 17—Never stop praying          God's will for you
• Verse 18—Never stop giving thanks

**(C)** *Step Four*—Cross reference each of the verses with another similar idea in the Bible. The best commentary on Scripture is Scripture. Look for verses that will help explain, illustrate, or in some way clarify the idea.

### 1 THESSALONIANS 5:16-18

- Verse 16—Philippians 4:4
- Verse 17—Ephesians 6:18
- Verse 18—Romans 1:21; Ephesians 5:20

**(A)** *Step Five*—Choose from the possible applications the one God would have you work on, stating the problem, an example of the problem, the solution, and the specific thing God would have you do to apply the solution.

### 1 THESSALONIANS 5:16-18

- Verse 18—I am convicted by the fact I am unthankful. Just yesterday I realized that I had not thanked my wife for all the hard work she does in cooking, keeping house, taking care of the children, and many other things.
- I purpose before God to begin checking this ingratitude and replacing it with verbal expressions of thanksgiving.
- I will apologize to the Lord and to my wife and ask their forgiveness.
- Each day this week I will ask God's help in this during my morning devotions and seek to implement it during the day.
- I will talk this over with my children and ask them to call to my attention any failures to express gratitude to my wife.

Do not go on to the Advanced section until you have mastered these five basic steps.

## Advanced Verse Analysis

After you have done the above study for a period of time, feel comfortable with it, and want to proceed further, you may try the next four steps. Bible study should not become burdensome or complicated. Don't add these steps prematurely to your study. Nor should you feel "less spiritual" if you never add them. Methodology must always be your servant, never your master.

**(I)** *Step Six*—Select the pivotal idea in the passage. This is the word or phrase around which the thought moves. Ask yourself, *Is the principal thrust of this passage to exhort to some action or to teach a doctrine?* If action, then concentrate on the verbs. The key is likely to be found there. If doctrine, concentrate on the nouns.

### 1 THESSALONIANS 5:16-18

- Verse 17—The pivotal word is *pray*. It is the *means* of appropriating God's grace enabling you to *rejoice*. *Giving thanks* is the *method* of prayer.

**(I)** *Step Seven*—In one sentence write the distilled essence or theme of the passage. Tie the verses together into one "big idea."

### 1 THESSALONIANS 5:16-18

- God's will for the believer is that in prayer he thanks God for all circumstances so as to rejoice perpetually.

**(C)** *Step Eight*—Chart the passage, seeking to draw the parts into a whole and relating them to one another. The various methods of chart making are outlined in Chapter 10.

## 1 THESSALONIANS 5:16-18

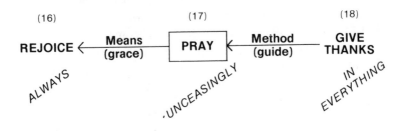

**(I)** *Step Nine*—Choose a title for the passage

1 THESSALONIANS 5:16-18

- *Title:* "The Will of God in Christ Jesus for Me"

# 3 The Analytical Method of Bible Study

To analyze something is to study the object in detail, being careful to note even the most minute aspects. This is the objective of analytical Bible study. Here we seek to examine a passage carefully and thoroughly. The purpose is to understand what the writer had in mind when he wrote to his audience.

In many ways the analytical method can be contrasted with the synthetic method of Bible study, which is the topic of Chapter 4. In the synthetic study you will look at the larger picture, as through a telescope. Here in the analytical method you

25

study the parts as through a microscope. Using the illustration of a library, in the synthetic approach you are looking at the composition of the library, while in the analytic approach you are studying the contents of each book.

Analytical Bible study is the "meat and potatoes" of your study of Scripture. As the years progress, you will, in all probability, lean on it as the mainstay of your Bible study program. It is basic for a thorough knowledge of the Word, allowing the student opportunity to interface with why the writer said what he did the way he did. Again, the objective is to reconstruct as clearly as possible the original thinking of the writer.

Question-and-answer Bible studies are a form of the analytical method, as is the verse analysis method presented in Chapter 2. The study on which we are about to embark will launch you into studying a whole passage on your own.

As in verse analysis, a letter indicating the part you are doing is noted next to each of the steps to draw attention to the four basic parts of Bible study.

(O) OBSERVATION
(I) INTERPRETATION
(C) CORRELATION
(A) APPLICATION

As you become increasingly proficient in your use of the analytical method, you may want to refer to the individual chapters dealing with these parts for additional help.

## Basic Analytical Study

For the purpose of illustration, 1 Peter 2 will be the chapter analyzed in walking through the procedure.

(O) *Step One*—Read through the passage carefully. Take a sheet of paper and mark OBSERVATIONS on the top. This will be used throughout the study. Include on this sheet:

1. Observations—Note any and every detail you notice. Bombard the passage with questions such as who? what? where? when? why? and how? Note nouns, verbs, and other key words.

2. Problems—Write out what you don't understand about the passage. Don't say, "I don't understand verse 4." Rather, elaborate on what it is you don't understand. Some of your questions will resolve themselves as you continue your study. Others will be resolved only by referring to an outside source such as your pastor or a commentary. Some of your questions may never be answered.

3. Cross-references—Using the book *Treasury of Scripture Knowledge* or the marginal references in your Bible, cross reference the word, quote, or idea with a similar text elsewhere in the Bible. This will help in your understanding of the passage.

4. Possible applications—You will observe several of these in the course of your study. Note them on this sheet with an (A) in the margin. At the conclusion of your study you will return to these possible applications and select the one on which the Holy Spirit will have you focus.

The following is a sample list of observations taken from 1 Peter 2. They are all listed in this illustration, but you should remember that the list is *not* completed in *Step One* before going on to *Step Two*. You will be adding to the observations throughout the entire study. Don't be concerned that the observations be sequential. If you are half way through the chapter, and have a fresh thought about verse 1, note it right there. Don't worry about trying to squeeze it in at the top of the page.

### 1 Peter 2 — Observations

(I) • Verse 1—To follow this advice is to become alienated from the world, for this is how the world acts. Not to follow it is to be alienated from God.

(C) • Verse 3—Psalm 34:8.

(O) • Verses 1, 11—Sanctification is one of the emphases of 1 Peter. It must be in three directions: (1) toward God

(1:13)—hope, have faith, appropriate God's grace; (2) toward others (2:1)—related to the last six of the Ten Commandments; and (3) toward self (2:11)—these are sins that primarily hurt the person committing them.

**(O)** • Verses 4-8—Three quotes from the Old Testament are used to explain the use of *stone* in reference to Jesus Christ (Isaiah 28:16; Psalm 118:22; Isaiah 8:14).

**(O)** • Verses 9-10—Who are we? We are a . . .

—*Chosen people*—the word *chosen* is also used in 1:2. We have been chosen to obedience (1:2), and we have been chosen for service (2:9). Sanctification is our goal and obedience is the process.

—*Royal priesthood*—in verse 5 it was a *holy* priesthood; here it is a *royal* one, with the imagery probably taken from Melchizedek, the king-priest in the Old Testament (Genesis 14).

—*Holy nation*—collectively we are the people of God and form a unique nation, one that has holiness as its hallmark. Our goal is not to be like the world, but to be like Jesus Christ.

—*Peculiar people* (KJV)—we are a people especially suited for God to possess. The older expression *peculiar* means ''to bring about or obtain for oneself.'' God has obtained us to be a people for Himself.

**(A)**        —We were not always those four things, so we should praise God because He has changed us:

1. From darkness to light—from sin to glorious salvation.

2. From being no people to God's people—from insignificance to purpose and meaning.

3. From receiving no mercy to having mercy in abundance—we do not have to face judgment for our sins.

**(A)** • Verse 13—"every authority instituted among men." We must obey every law that does not violate God's laws whether the government is favorable or hostile, and we do it for the Lord's sake (see Acts 4:19; 5:25).

**(O)** • Verses 15, 19-20—the *two reasons* given in this section for submission and serving are: (1) demonstrate to the world that God's call is to a life of good and not evil; and (2) God is pleased with such conduct, since it is a reflection of the character of Jesus Christ (see verses 21-25).

**(O)** • Verses 13, 15—the two commands given in this section are *submit* and *serve*.

**(O)** • Verses 13-14, 18—the two groups to whom we are to submit and whom we are to serve are the *government* and *employers*.

**(O)** • Verses 13-20—possible outline for this section: "Submissive Servants—the Example of the Believer to the World."
1. Divine Despotism (verse 16)—proper perspective
2. Demonstration (verse 17)—proper attitude
3. Divine Directive (verses 13, 18)—proper life style
4. Two Groups (verses 13-14, 18)
5. Two Reasons (verses 15, 19-20)

**(O)** • Verse 25—we are very much like straying sheep, but Christ has brought us back to Himself. He is shown to be:

—*the Shepherd*—one of the oldest descriptions of God in the Bible (see Isaiah 40:11). He took care of His sheep—His people—even better than a shepherd in Judea took care of his sheep—the animals.

—*the Overseer*—this word means one who presides over, guards and protects. This is what Christ is to His people (see Matthew 28:20).

The observations in this section will vary in length, depending on how much time you are able to give to the study. Don't become discouraged if you don't "observe" much the first few times you do the study. With practice your observations will increase in number and in depth.

**(I)** *Step Two*—Take another sheet of paper and divide it in two parts, leaving ⅔ of the space on the left and ⅓ on the right. On the *far* left, write numerals down the page according to the number of verses in the chapter (25 for 1 Peter 2). On the left ⅔ of the sheet, verse by verse, state the key thought, that is, the main teaching, subject, or thought the writer is communicating in the content of the verse. (At times you may have difficulty verbalizing the key thoughts of certain verses, such as 1 Peter 2:1.)

On the remaining ⅓ of the sheet, try to combine the key thoughts of the verses into summary key thoughts. Try to feel the flow of the writer's argument. As you combine verses, it will become apparent where the paragraph divisions in the chapter are located.

It is important to note the flow of ideas in a passage—the relationship of the verses to one another. Sometimes the writer makes a general statement, then explains it with examples (see 2 Timothy 3:1-5). At other times he may list a series of ideas and then summarize with a general statement (see James 2:14-17). Or he may give a command, warning, or advice and back them up with reasons, purposes, or proofs. Try to determine what it is the writer is doing in the presentation of his material. Note the way he moves from one idea to the next. See Figure 1 for an example of 1 Peter 2.

**(I)** *Step Three*—Take a third sheet of paper and place it next to the sheet used in *Step Two*. You are now ready to begin tying the chapter together.

Looking at your *Summary of Key Thoughts* (right ⅓ of the

# 1 PETER 2 — KEY THOUGHTS AND SUMMARIES

| VERSE | KEY THOUGHTS | SUMMARY OF KEY THOUGHTS |
|---|---|---|
| 1. | Put away your sin | |
| 2. | Like babies, crave the milk of the Word | 1-3 Put away sin; take in the Word |
| 3. | Assuming you have tasted God's goodness | |
| 4. | Come to God's rejected Stone — Christ | |
| 5. | You are a living stone to God's honor | |
| 6. | The O.T. tells us to believe in The Cornerstone | 4-8 Like a cornerstone, Christ is built on or rejected |
| 7. | Unbelievers have rejected God's Cornerstone | |
| 8. | In their disobedience they stumble over Him | |
| 9. | God has chosen you to proclaim Christ | 9-10 You once rejected Christ, but are now His |
| 10. | Once you were outside of Christ, but are now His | |
| 11. | Stay away from fleshly desires | 11-12 Holiness is the best testimony |
| 12. | Let the uncommitted glorify God for your deeds | |
| 13. | Obey the laws of the land | |
| 14. | The law punishes the bad and praises the good | |
| 15. | Let your good silence those who condemn the Gospel | 13-17 Believers as free men are to obey the law and love others |
| 16. | Use your freedom for good, not evil | |
| 17. | Love others — fear God | |
| 18. | Servants are to obey their masters | |
| 19. | God will reward the servant whose master is cruel | 18-20 Servants are to submit — even to cruel masters |
| 20. | You are specially rewarded when suffering for good | |
| 21. | In this you are to follow Christ's example | |
| 22. | Christ was sinless | |
| 23. | When punished for good, He did not retaliate | 21-25 Christ's response to rejection is our example |
| 24. | His suffering was punishment for our sins | |
| 25. | Like wandering sheep you have returned to Him | |

Figure 1

previous sheet), divide the chapter into its paragraphs. These are easily determined by the natural breaks in the writer's flow of thought.

Write a key thought for each paragraph. The key thought for each paragraph will be a combining of all summary statements on that paragraph. Likewise, the key thought of the chapter will be a summary of the key thought of your paragraphs. What you are doing here is funneling the passage in such a way as to distill its essential meaning (see Figure 3). The key thought for the paragraph is the distilled essence of that paragraph in one sentence and the key thought of the chapter is the distilled essence of the chapter in one sentence. Make each of these sentences as brief as possible without sacrificing the main truth.

You can take each paragraph and put subpoints under it. This is especially helpful if the paragraph(s) tend to be long. This is an optional part of *Step Three*.

### 1 PETER 2 — OUTLINE

I. Verses 1-10—By studying the Word of God, the Christian is to reflect the character of Christ, who is God's cornerstone, rejected by men.
   A. Strip off the world; drink in the Word (verses 1-3)
   B. Stone of stumbling or salvation (verses 4-8)
   C. Showcase of contrast (verses 9-10)

II. Verses 11-25—Christ set an example for the Christians on how to respond to a world that does not know Him.
   A. Sanctified living is the best testimony (verses 11-12)
   B. Submission—the Christian's example to the world (verses 13-20)
   C. Submission—Christ's example to the believer (verses 21-25)

(A) *Step Four*—Choose from the possible applications the one God would have you work on: stating the problem, an example of the problem, the solution, and the specific things God would have you do to apply the solution.

1 Peter 2—Application

- Verse 13—"Submit yourselves for the Lord's sake to every authority instituted among men." The Lord has spoken to me regarding my habitually exceeding the speed laws. When I drive my auto, I almost always go faster than the speed limit.

  For example, the other day I was on my way downtown and caught myself with one eye looking ahead and the other behind, to see if I would be caught speeding by the police. I know the Lord would have me slow down.
- More often than not, I speed because I am late for an appointment. This happens because of laziness on my part. To make application, I will:
    1. Ask the Lord's forgiveness.
    2. Declare myself on this issue to my family and friends, and ask that they remind me when I exceed the law.
    3. Leave early for every appointment, so I won't have the pressure of disobeying the "authority instituted among men."

Do not go on to the Advanced section until you have mastered these four basic steps.

## Advanced Analytical Study

If, after doing these four steps for a period of time, you want to add to your study, you can do two things. One is to read Chapters 8–11 and implement those parts of observation, interpretation, correlation, and application that apply to these four steps of the basic study. The other is to add further steps to your study. Be bold and imaginative in this. Try new things. Methods are designed to help you, not enslave you. Put aside what doesn't work for you and add what does. Remember, the objective of Bible study is to determine the meaning of the writer at the time he wrote it, and apply this truth to your life. Everything else is methodology to help you in this quest.

The following are five other steps you can add if and when you feel ready.

(I) *Step Five*—Select the pivotal idea in the passage. This is the word or phrase around which the thought of the passage moves. Ask yourself, *Is the flow of the passage in the direction of exhortation to action, or teaching doctrine?* If action, then concentrate on the verbs. The pivotal idea is likely to be found there. If the flow of the passage is on teaching doctrine, then concentrate on the nouns.

On a separate sheet of paper make two columns. List the key verbs in one and the key nouns in the other, verse by verse. Study these lists and determine if the thrust of the chapter is in the direction of action or doctrine.

Look for the appropriate verb or noun (or perhaps phrase) that is amplified in some respect in each paragraph of the passage. This is the pivotal idea. If there is more than one that qualifies, then choose the best one.

After studying these parallel bits in Figure 2, you can see that 1 Peter 2 is an exhortation to action. From the important verbs listed, the key ones are circled. Peter's exhortation is to follow His (Christ's) example (verse 21). "Follow His Example," then, is the pivotal idea of the passage.

(I) *Step Six*—The *key thought of the passage* is the essence of the passage in one sentence. The key thought of each paragraph is how the writer develops that passage. This was determined in *Step Three.* By now you have discovered that finding the *pivotal idea (Step Five)* is helpful in determining the *key thought of the pas-*

# 1 PETER 2 — PIVOTAL IDEA

| VERSE | VERBS | NOUNS |
|---|---|---|
| 1. | rid (yourselves) | malice, deceit, hypocrisy, jealousy, slander |
| 2. | crave, grow | babies, milk (Word, S.C.), salvation |
| 3. | taste | Lord, good |
| 4. | come | Stone |
| 5. | are being built offering, acceptable | stones, house, priesthood, sacrifices |
| 6. | trusts | cornerstone |
| 7. | believe, rejected | stone, builders, capstone |
| 8. | causes, makes, stumble | stone, rock, message |
| 9. | you are, declare | people, priesthood, nation, darkness, light |
| 10. | were not, (now) are | people, God, mercy |
| 11. | abstain | (sinful) desires, soul |
| 12. | live, see | (good) lives, deeds |
| 13. | submit | authority, king |
| 14. | | governors |
| 15. | | |
| 16. | | |
| 17. | show . . . respect, love, fear | |
| 18. | submit (yourselves) | slaves, masters |
| 19. | bears up | commendable, God |
| 20. | suffer | |
| 21. | (you) were called, follow | Christ, example |
| 22. | | |
| 23. | | |
| 24. | | |
| 25. | | Shepherd, Overseer |

Figure 2

*sage,* which we will elaborate on here in *Step Six.* This whole process is illustrated in Figure 3.

## THE FLOW OF THE WRITER'S ARGUMENT

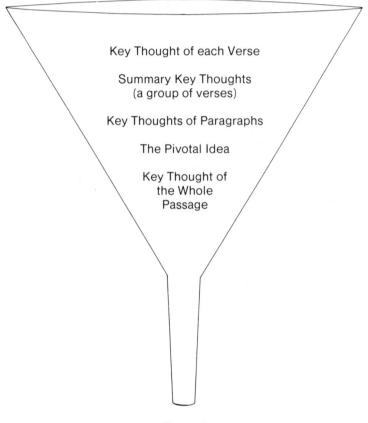

Key Thought of each Verse

Summary Key Thoughts
(a group of verses)

Key Thoughts of Paragraphs

The Pivotal Idea

Key Thought of
the Whole
Passage

Figure 3

The *key thought of the passage* should then be developed as the eminent truth of the passage. In doing so, state the *key thought of the passage* at the beginning and end of your eminent truth. The development of the key thought of the passage is the articulation of the writer's message and follows the flow of the passage (see Figure 3 above). You can have only *one* key thought to the passage. Each person doing a study may state it in his own words, but it should become immediately apparent in a comparison of key thoughts written by various people that they are all studying the same passage. A correct application of the above six steps should lead everyone to the same conclusion. This is illustrated in Figure 4.

## I Peter 2 — Key Thought of the Passage

The Christian is called on to follow the example of Christ into a life of submission and suffering at the hands of a hostile world.

### EMINENT TRUTH

The Christian is called on to follow the example of Christ and live a life of submission and suffering at the hands of a hostile world.

The holiness of Jesus Christ was such a contrast to a sinful world that men either had to conform to Him or destroy Him. Peter uses the illustration of a cornerstone. The cornerstone properly laid insured that the building would be straight and solid. Prior to Christ all "buildings" (lives of people) were crooked. The contrast wasn't seen till Christ the perfect "building" appeared. He was rejected and crucified (verses 4-8).

Christ's suffering and rejection was *caused* by the sinfulness of man and *resulted* in the salvation of man. His death on the cross (verse 24) paid the penalty for sin and brought a solution to man's problem.

All of this was possible, however, because Christ understood His role and was submissive to it (verses 22-23). So we also must understand our roles and be submissive to them. Our holiness (verses 1, 9, 11, and others), like Christ's, evokes a negative reaction from a sinful world (verse 20). Thus sinful men persecute us just as they did Him. Our response must be to *serve* and *submit*. This example will aid in God's plan of redemption (verses 12, 15). In short, we are to *follow His example* (verse 21).

The Christian is called on to follow the example of Christ into a life of submission and suffering at the hands of a hostile world.

Figure 4

AN EXAMPLE TO FOLLOW

| | 2:1-3 | 2:4-8 | 2:9-10 | 2:11-12 | 2:13-20 | 2:21-25 |
|---|---|---|---|---|---|---|
| | GROW | COME | DECLARE | ABSTAIN | SUBMIT | FOLLOW |
| | SANCTIFIED TO GROW | CHRIST REJECTED | WHO WE ARE | SANCTIFIED TO BEHOLD | HOW WE OUGHT TO LIVE | CHRIST'S RESPONSE TO REJECTION |

DESTINY — — — BE SUBMISSIVE — — — DUTY

FOR YOUR OWN SAKE — — — FOR THE SAKE OF THE WORLD

CHRIST THE STONE — — — CHRIST THE SHEPHERD

Figure 5

(I) *Step Seven*—Write a title for each paragraph and then for the whole chapter (or passage). The purpose of a title is *identification*. It is a tool to help you recall the passage and its contents. Here is where you can show your creativity, and may want to use something catchy.

> 1 PETER 2—TITLE
> "An Example to Follow"

Figure 6

(C) *Step Eight*—Charting a passage is a way of relating the part to the whole and comparing the various parts with one another. Read Chapter 5, which explains the various techniques for charting, and chart the passage you have just studied. See Figure 5 for an example.

(O) *Step Nine*—For the truly ambitious, a ninth and final step you may incorporate is to memorize the passage. Though such a task is hard work, it pays rich rewards. As you review the passage, fresh observations and insights will come to mind which you can add to your *Observation* section *(Step One)*. The following suggestions are for your consideration.

1. Memorize from only one translation. Use the one from which you are studying.

2. Place the verses on cards—one verse per card—putting the verse on one side and the reference on the other. (Blank cards specifically designed for this may be obtained from your local Christian bookstore, or by writing Customer Services, NavPress, P.O. Box 20, Colorado Springs, Colorado 80901; 1,000 cards for $2.50.)

3. Review, *Review*, REVIEW. Few things are as frustrating as memorizing a portion of Scripture and then forgetting it. Review is hard work, but keep current in it.

4. Memorize the passage *before* you begin your study. This will help you in every step you employ. It will tie the passage into a unit and give you the ability to have the whole in mind as you study it verse by verse.

Do not allow the methodology to overwhelm you. For example, in the five advanced steps, choose only those with which you feel comfortable. In time you may want to design a new step and use it. There is nothing sacred about methodology. Its value lies in its ability to help you become a more proficient student of the Word of God.

# 4 The Synthetic Method of Bible Study

**SYNTHETIC STUDY**

**The broad, overall study of a book of the Bible.**

The synthetic method of Bible study approaches each book of the Bible as a unit and seeks to understand its meaning as a whole. The objective is to get a broad, panoramic view of the book. It does not concern itself with details but the overall scope of the book.

In the analytical method you looked at the text through a microscope. In the synthetic method you look at it through a telescope. What did the writer, moved by the Holy Spirit, have in mind as he wrote? What is the key thought or big idea in the book? How does he make his point? These are the kinds of questions that are germaine to the synthetic method.

This method is probably the most difficult of all the Bible study methods, but can also prove to be the most rewarding.

As in every method of Bible study, you will incorporate four basic parts:

**(O)** OBSERVATION
**(I)** INTERPRETATION
**(C)** CORRELATION
**(A)** APPLICATION

Next to each step in the study you will note one of the above four letters. These are meant to alert you to the part employed in that step. Further information on how to approach each of these four parts may be found in Chapters 8–11.

## Basic Synthetic Study

For the purpose of illustration, the Book of Romans will be synthesized in walking through the procedure.

**(O)** *Step One*—Read through the book carefully. Take a sheet of paper and mark *Observations* on the top. This will be used throughout the entire study. Include on this sheet:

1. Observations—Note the key thoughts or main arguments that flow through the book. List the important words. Note such things as places, events, and important names. List things you may want to study later.

2. Problems—When you are unable to follow the thinking of the writer, note when this occurs and exactly what it is you don't understand.

3. Cross-references—Note any important events or quotes the writer uses from other parts of the Bible. For example, Romans 10:18-21 refers to a series of quotes from the Old Testament (Psalm 19:4; Deuteronomy 32:21; Isaiah 65:1-2). An understanding of the context of each of those quotes will help you discover the flow of Paul's argument in the Book of Romans.

4. Possible Applications—Several of these will come to your attention as you read and reread the book. Note these for use later in your study.

Figure 7 is a sample list of observations taken from the Book of Romans. They are all listed on one page, but it should be remembered that the *Observations* are *not* completed in *Step One* before going on to *Step Two*. Rather, use this sheet throughout the entire study and add to it as you go along.

**(I)** *Step Two*—Read the book through a second time, involving yourself in a process of intensive exploration. Your objective is to unravel the writer's argument. As you read, list under your *Observations* the key thoughts or major themes of the book. Try to put them in your own words. Don't let the chapter and verse divisions destroy the unity of the book, for these divisions were not there when the writer penned his book originally. Be sure to do this reading in one sitting.

(The illustration of *Step Two* is included in *Step One* in Figure 7.)

**(I)** *Step Three*—Read the book carefully a third time. Ask the Holy Spirit to enable you to approach it with a fresh mind. With a pen in your hand complete your reading in one sitting.

As you read this time, look for the main theme or big idea the writer is communicating. This is the key thought of the book—the organizing principle that gives the book its unity.

Is there any particular place in the book where the key thought is mentioned? Does any one verse or passage state the idea more succinctly than any other? If so, note this.

As you compare this key thought with the themes listed in *Step Two,* the unity should become apparent. Write the key thought out in your own words.

# ROMANS — Observations

VERSE                          OBSERVATIONS

1:18        Paul begins his epistle by establishing the fact of man's sin. He deals first with the world at large (1:18-32), then the moralist (2:1-16), and finally the Jew (2:17 – 3:9).

3:21-26     Here we see the solution to our problem—the death of Christ—a beautiful, logical flow in Paul's teaching.

2:7         What does this mean? Is Paul here saying that a person can *work* his way to heaven?

3:1         The Jews had a tremendous advantage. So do I as a man
(**A**)     born in a Christian heritage. I should list all the advantages I have that much of the world does not.

4:1         Why does Paul talk about Abraham after Christ?

5:12-21     What is the gist of Paul's argument in this passage? What is he seeking to communicate?

6:1-4       A beautiful picture of our identification with Christ in His death, burial, and resurrection.

Whole       Outline:
            1. Man's need (1:1 – 3:20)
            2. God's solution (3:21 – 5:21)
            3. Implication for Christians (6:1 – 8:39)
            4. Implication for Jews (9:1 – 11:36)
            5. Application (12:1 – 16:27)

9:3         Paul wished himself accursed" from Christ for his kinsmen.
(**A**)     Do I have that kind of love for people?—a real challenge!

11:1-32     Paul seems to indicate that there will be a future for Israel? Is this for the nation or just certain individuals? What does "ALL" in verse 26 mean?

12:19       "Avenge not yourself"—I find that I tend to be vindictive
(**A**)     toward people who I feel have wronged me.

13:2        Does this passage imply that the thirteen colonies were wrong in declaring their independence from Britain in 1776?

14:1-23     This is a passage on Christian liberties. It has far-reaching implication for the church today. Note the question and answer method Paul uses in communicating.

Figure 7

ROMANS—KEY THOUGHT

Romans 1:16-17—*The just shall live by faith.*

(C) *Step Four*—Read the entire book a fourth time. Approach your reading as though you are exploring the book for the very first time. Don't "breeze" through it. Again, do this reading at one sitting. Be sure and set aside adequate time so as not to be interrupted.

This time through, develop a broad outline of the book. Be more interested in the flow of the writer's thinking than the chapter divisions. Resist the temptation to use the outline found in many study Bibles. This is *your* exploration, so get your own outline.

Title the various divisions in your outline and write a title for the book.

ROMANS—OUTLINE

A Christian Catechism

  I. Doctrine, 1:1–5:21
      A. Introduction, 1:1-17
      B. Man's Problem, 1:18–3:20
      C. God's Solution, 3:21–5:21
 II. Implication, 6:1–11:36
      A. Believers, 6:1–8:39, . . .
          1. and sin, 6:1-23
          2. and the law, 7:1-25
          3. delivered, 8:1-39
      B. Jews, 9:1–11:36
          1. A sovereign choice, 9:1-33
          2. A universal message, 10:1-21
          3. A future for Israel, 11:1-36
III. Application, 12:1–16:27
      A. The Believer and the Church, 12:1-21
      B. The Believer and the World, 13:1-14
      C. The Believer and Christian Liberty, 14:1–15:7
      D. Future Plans and Closing Remarks, 15:8–16:27

**(O)** *Step Five*—Summarize the historical background on the book. You can derive much of this information from the book itself; for some of it you will have to consult Bible study aids, such as, *Zondervan's Pictorial Dictionary of the Bible* (5 volumes), *Eerdmans Bible Handbook,* and *Halley's Bible Handbook.*

Try to determine the following:

1. Who wrote the book? How is the writer presented in the book? What does he reveal about himself?
2. To whom was the book written? Where did they live? What was the geography like and what kind of people were they?
3. When and where was it written? What circumstances and environment surrounded the writer as he wrote?
4. Why was the book written? What was on the writer's mind when he sat down to write? Were there any special problems that occasioned the writing? Is the book designed to communicate a particular thing?

### ROMANS—BACKGROUND

1. The letter begins by claiming to be written by Paul (1:1). When the writer describes his ministry later on (Chapter 15), it sounds like Paul. The ideas, style of the letter, and vocabulary all support the claim that Paul wrote it.

   The church fathers and others through the centuries all refer to Paul as the writer.

   Having never visited Rome on his missionary journeys, Paul communicates a warmth and acceptance of the Romans (1:4-12); he states that his contact with them will be *mutually* edifying.

2. Many theories exist as to how the Church at Rome got started (such as, the Apostle Peter founded it), but the best is that it was started by Jews from Rome converted on the day of Pentecost (see Acts 2). Many Jews lived in Rome, having been taken there when Palestine was conquered by Rome in 63 B.C.

3. Paul says he has finished the first phase of his ministry and is ready to move on into Spain (see 15:22). He wants to visit Rome on his way, traveling first to Jerusalem.

   Phoebe is mentioned in this letter (16:1), and she was from Corinth. This, along with other evidence, indicates that Corinth was the city from which Paul wrote Romans. It was written during his third journey, about A.D. 57-58.

4. Since Paul had never ministered in Rome, there were no special problems that confronted him. He wanted to introduce himself to the church and gain their support for his further missionary activity in Spain.

   Some say he wanted to reconcile differences that existed between the Jews and Gentiles, but more probably he simply wanted to set forth a compendium of his thoughts on the theology of the gospel.

**(A)** *Step Six*—Choose from the possible applications listed in your *Observations* the one on which God would have you work. Suggestions on how to do this are found in Chapter 11.

Do not go to the Advanced section until  you have mastered these six basic steps.

## Advanced Synthetic Study

If, after doing these steps for a period of time you want to add to your study, you can go two routes. One is to read Chapters 8–11 and implement those parts that apply to these steps. The other is to add further steps of your own. Be bold and imaginative. Try new things. Method is designed to help you, not enslave you. Put aside what doesn't work for you and add what does. The objective of Bible study is to determine the meaning of the writer at the time he wrote it, and apply this truth to your life. Everything else is methodology to help you in this quest. Three more steps are suggested here.

**(I)** *Step Seven*—Study the format of the book to determine the style the writer uses. The following are examples of what to look for in the book you are studying.

1. Topical—Here the writer deals with certain topics. The Gospel of Matthew is an example. Matthew sets forth the life of Christ in topical fashion.

2. Chronological—Here the writer relates a sequence of events and a story unfolds. An example of this style are in the books of 1 and 2 Kings, which originally were one book.

3. Apologetic—Here in polemic form the writer argues his point. Galatians is a beautiful example of this. Paul dispenses with the usual niceties in his introduction and gets right down to business.

4. Interrogative—Here the writer, in making his point, jabs with probing questions. This is the style used by Malachi.

5. Logical—Here the writer systematically moves in such a way so as to lead us to his conclusion. This is Paul's style in the Book of Romans. He begins with the universal fact of sin, systematically destroying any argument for self-recovery in the process, and leads us to the foot of the cross. His method is that of using questions and answers, much like the techniques used in catechism instruction.

**(C)** *Step Eight*—Chart the book. This will prove to be a helpful step in viewing the book as a unit and comparing the parts with one another. For assistance in how to do this, turn to Chapter 10. Study the example in Figure 8.

**(I)** *Step Nine*—Determine the place of the book in the Bible as a whole. Each book has its own unique contribution to the whole of the Bible. What would be missing if this book were omitted?

## ROMANS – A CHRISTIAN CATECHISM

| | Doctrine | | | | | | | | | Implication | | | Application | | | |
|---|---|---|---|---|---|---|---|---|---|---|---|---|---|---|---|---|
| 1:1-17 | 1:18-2:16 | 2:17-3:20 | 3:21-31 | 4:1-25 | 5:1-21 | 6:1-23 | 7:1-25 | 8:1-39 | 9:1-33 | 10:1-21 | 11:1-36 | 12:1-21 | 13:1-14 | 14:1-15:7 | 15:8-16:27 |
| Introduction | The Unbeliever and Sin | The Unbeliever and the Law | The Unbeliever Delivered | Deliverance in the OT III. – Abraham | The Doctrine of Imputation Elaborated | The Believer and Sin | The Believer and the Law | The Believer Delivered | A Sovereign Choice | A Universal Message | A Future for Israel | The Believer and the Church | The Believer and the World | The Believer and Christian Liberty | Future Plans and Closing Remarks |
| | SIN — MAN Unbeliever in Sin | | SALVATION — GOD (God the Son) | | | SANCTIFICATION — MAN-GOD (HS) Believer in Sin | | | SELECTION — GOD (God the Father) | | | SERVICE — MAN | | | |
| | LIFE BY FAITH | | | | | | | | | | | SERVICE BY FAITH | | | |
| | Slave to Sin | | Slave to God | | | Slave to God | | | | | | Slave Serving God | | | |
| | HIS Righteousness IN LAW | | HIS Righteousness IMPUTED | | | HIS Righteousness OBEYED | | | HIS Righteousness IN ELECTION | | | HIS Righteousness DISPLAYED | | | |
| | The Need of Salvation | | The Way of Salvation | | | The Life of Salvation | | | The Scope of Salvation | | | The Service of Salvation | | | |

Figure 8

### ROMANS—ITS CONTRIBUTION

Many believe Romans to be the greatest of the New Testament books. It certainly is the most thorough presentation of the ''whole counsel of God.'' It forms the basis of the great theological works written through the ages and it was the major book of the Protestant Reformation.

In contrast to the other religions of the world, which are religions of achievement, Christianity is a religion of rescue. Romans is the clearest presentation of this fact of all the New Testament documents.

## Conclusion

Ideally the synthetic method should be used in conjunction with the analytic method. View the book as a whole, then look at its parts, and finally reexamine the whole. Diagramed, it would look like this:

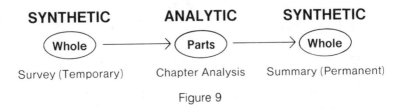

Figure 9

Applying this method means you do a synthetic study first, as described in this chapter. Then do a chapter by chapter analysis of the book described in the preceding chapter. Finally, repeat the synthetic study of the book. This final study will either confirm or invalidate the first synthetic study.

If you elect to do this, be careful to approach your second synthetic study with an open, fresh mind. Put your first study aside and don't refer to it till you are all done. Then bring it out for purposes of comparison.

This is a step that should only be taken by a seasoned Bible student. Do not tackle more than you can handle, as it leads to frustration, discouragement, and ultimately quitting. If, as you implement these steps, you find you are doing too much, back away from the new material. You are not in competition with anyone. Later, if you feel up to it, give it another try. If you decide never to try, fine!

# 5 The Topical Method of Bible Study

In Paul's Epistle to the Romans he introduces a number of different topics and weaves them together into the message he is communicating. Examples of these topics are faith, grace, justification, Holy Spirit, and sin. His treatment of each of these topics is not complete, but it does give you some insights into how God feels about them.

This is true for all the writers of the Bible. Each touches on a host of topics in making his point.

In the topical method of Bible study you "chase" a selected topic through the Bible. How far you chase it will depend on the time you have and your overall objective. For the average student, the larger the topic the more narrow the study will have to be.

For example, the study of *sin* in the Bible would promise to be a gargantuan task. Even a study of *Jesus' teaching on sin* would be huge. Either you will have to avoid subjects of this size, or narrow them down still further, like, *John's teaching of sin in his first letter*.

A smaller topic can be treated much more broadly. If, for example, you decide to study the word *victory* in the Bible, you can search all 66 books, and find that in the whole Bible it only appears 11 times.

Sometimes the topic being studied has synonyms: law, statutes, commands, ordinances, precepts, testimonies are all used interchangeably in the Psalms. For this reason, a topical or cyclopedic index can often prove more useful than a concordance. The *Thompson Chain Reference Bible* is excellent for this, as is Thomas Nelson's *The Open Bible* Edition. *Strong's* and *Young's* concordances are two exhaustive ones from which to choose. *Nave's Topical Bible* is still another.

As in the Verse Analysis method, to draw attention to the four basic parts of Bible study, a letter indicating the part you are doing is noted next to each of the steps.

**(O)** OBSERVATION
**(I)** INTERPRETATION
**(C)** CORRELATION
**(A)** APPLICATION

## Basic Topical Study

For purposes of illustration, we will use the word *hospitality* as our topic for study.

**(C)** *Step One*—Choose the word to be studied and the boundaries of the study, such as a book, section of Bible, or the whole Bible. Write out the purpose or objective of the study. Using a Bible study aid such as those listed above, locate the references to be included in your study. On a sheet of paper list these references vertically using the left hand side of the sheet.

HOSPITALITY—TOPIC, PURPOSE, AND REFERENCES

*Topic to Be Studied:* HOSPITALITY
*Purpose of the Study:* To learn the biblical concept of hospitality, so that we might use our home as the Bible teaches.
*References:*

> Matthew 25:35
> Luke 7:44-46
> Luke 11:5-8
> Romans 12:13
> 1 Timothy 3:2
> Titus 1:8
> Hebrews 13:2
> 1 Peter 4:9

**(O)** *Step Two*—Take a sheet of paper and mark *Observations* on the top. This will be used throughout the study. Include on this sheet:

1. Observations—Note any and every detail you notice. Bombard the references with questions such as: who? what? where? when? why? and how? Note the nouns, verbs, and other key words.

2. Problems—Write out what you don't understand about the references and topic. Don't say, "I don't understand Ephesians 4:8." Rather, elaborate on what it is you don't understand. Some of your questions will resolve themselves as you continue your study. Others will be resolved only by referring to outside sources such as your pastor or a commentary. Some of your questions may never be answered.

3. Possible application—you will observe several of these in the course of your study. Note them on this sheet with an **(A)** in the margin. At the conclusion of your study you will return to these possible applications and select the one on which the Holy Spirit will have you focus.

### HOSPITALITY—OBSERVATIONS

**(O)** • *Definitions:* Hospitality is "the reception and entertainment of strangers" *(The Open Bible)*.

*Hospitable* as entered in the dictionary listing is between *Hospice,* a place for a stranger to rest and lodge, and *Hospital,* a place to care for the sick. It means: "Given to generous and cordial reception of guests" *(Webster's New Collegiate Dictionary)*.

*Hospitality* is "hospitable treatment, reception, or disposition" *(Webster's New Collegiate Dictionary)*.

**(O)** • Matthew 25:35—Jesus' judgment on the nations for their acceptance or rejection of Him and His brethren in the context of provision.

—The bare essentials are listed: food, drink, shelter, clothing, and fellowship.

—Why is the emphasis placed on strangers? The church was dispersed and the traveling believer could find acceptance and provision in the context of the local body of believers; therefore, the saints were to expect strangers. Also they never knew when they might be entertaining angels (Hebrews 13:2).

**(A)** —My tendency is to entertain those I *know,* rather than provide for the stranger.

**(O)** • Luke 7:44-46—Jesus contrasts the entertaining host and the hospitable stranger. The host did not provide any courtesies to his guest, while the stranger provided water, greeting, and anointing.

—Jesus reveals that a person's motives are reflected in whether hospitality is given out of love or obligation.

—What are the courtesies of hospitality in my culture today? A welcome greeting, something to drink, communicating an interest in the guest, food, and other amenities.

—Contrast Simon to Martha and Mary, who eagerly received Jesus into their home (Luke 10:38; John 12:2).

(O) • Luke 11:5-8—There is a cost in meeting the needs of others: inconvenience (the hour was late and the family settled for the night), time, and provision.

—Because of a friendship (relationship), the person felt free to go to him for help in a time of need.

—Hospitality is meeting the needs of others, not merely entertaining guests as our culture portrays. Cultural entertaining to show off our skills as cooks, tidy homekeepers, or the array of such things as china, silver, and art objects, is opposite of the biblical teaching on hospitality.

(O) • Romans 12:13—The providing of needs and the commitment to hospitality are listed together.

—The believers are singled out as the recipients.

—Synonyms: given, committed, addicted (1 Corinthians 16:15 KJV).

—Hospitality isn't a decision making procedure but the reflection of a life style. The home isn't regarded as an ivory tower of retreat for themselves but a hospice for service to others.

**(O)** • 1 Timothy 3:2—What does it mean to be given to hospitality? The word *given* connotes more than something you take or leave, but a way of life, a life style.

—In Genesis 18, Sarah and Abraham were not expecting guests, yet as the strangers approached, Abraham *ran* to meet them, greeted them by *bowing* to them, gave them *water* to wash their feet, and then had Sarah prepare a full meal. They went out of their way to make the strangers welcome. The cost to them was time, effort, and provisions. Yet there was no hesitation on their part, but an eager giving of themselves (see 2 Corinthians 8:5).

**(O)** • Titus 1:8—Church leaders must love hospitality.

—Hospitality cannot be separated from people and a concern and interest in them. It means giving myself to others because I am concerned for them.

**(O)** —In John 4, we see Jesus as a tired, hungry traveler. Yet He gave Himself to the Samaritan woman by talking with her, answering her questions, and offering her living water that would satisfy the deepest needs of her life. What a contrast to the response of the disciples, who were shocked that he would even speak to her!

**(O)** —2 Kings 4:8-10—A Shunammite couple with financial means prepared a room with a table, stool, lamp, and bed for the traveling prophet Elisha, so he might have a place to stay.

**(A)** • Hebrews 13:2—It is easy to become so involved in my own activities and friends that I neglect the stranger, such as visitors who attend church without my greeting them. If I did my part along with the rest of the congregation, "official greeters" wouldn't be necessary.

—Do angels still visit today?

—What are the Bible's accounts of people entertaining angels and not realizing who they were?

• Genesis 18:2-15—Abraham

• Genesis 19:1-22—Lot

• Judges 6:11-24—Gideon

• Judges 13:1-21—Samson's mother and father

—The angelic visitations were to convey a message, yet in each account they were entertained not because they were angels but because the people opened their homes and lives to strangers.

**(O)(C)** • 1 Peter 4:9—Because hospitality involves giving, the admonition of 2 Corinthians 9:7 applies: "Each person should give what he has decided in his heart to give, not reluctantly or under compulsion, for God loves a cheerful giver."

—Hospitality should reflect a heart attitude of eagerness, not the fulfillment of a duty. If I grasp the privilege of ministering to others by being hospitable, it removes the obligation and allows the Spirit of God to minister to others through me, which then becomes the reflection of a life style.

**(I)** *Step Three*—On the sheet used in *Step One* write out the *key thought* for each reference listed. The key thought is the distilled essence or main idea of the verse stated in your own words.

While doing *Step Three,* you should list many of your *observations* suggested in *Step Two.*

HOSPITALITY—KEY THOUGHTS

*Topic to Be Studied:* HOSPITALITY
*Purpose of the Study:* To learn the biblical concept of hospitality, so that we might use our home as the Bible teaches.
*References:*

Matthew 25:35—acceptance and provision for the stranger
Luke 7:44-46—to provide the courtesies of hospitality
Luke 11:5-8—cost involved in meeting others' needs
Romans 12:13—providing needs; committed to hospitality
1 Timothy 3:2—church leaders must be committed to hospitality
Titus 1:8—a lover of hospitality
Hebrews 13:2—entertain strangers; some have hosted angels
1 Peter 4:9—be hospitable without grudging

**(C)** *Step Four*—Arrange the verses into categories. The *key thoughts* listed in *Step Three* will help you select your categories. Ask yourself questions like, *What are the main categories suggested by these verses? How would I outline this subject to another person?* Some verses will fit under more than one category.

HOSPITALITY—CATEGORIES

Attitudes of hospitality
    1 Peter 4:9; Titus 1:8; 1 Timothy 3:2; Romans 12:13
Definition of hospitality
    Matthew 25:35; Luke 7:44-46; Romans 12:13
Costs and rewards of hospitality
    Luke 11:5-8; Hebrews 13:2

**(C)** *Step Five*—Outline the categories created in *Step Four,* listing the major divisions and important subdivisions. Place the key verses next to each division and subpoint.

Work for logical order and simplicity of structure. Don't make it complicated. Generally speaking, the simpler you make it the more you understand it. Constantly keep in mind the purpose of the study.

### HOSPITALITY—OUTLINE

I. Hospitality defined (Romans 12:13; Matthew 25:35-40)
II. Hospitality demonstrated (Luke 7:44-46)
- A. Attitudes toward hospitality (Titus 1:8, 1 Peter 4:9; 1 Timothy 3:2)
- B. Costs and benefits of hospitality (Luke 11:5-8; Hebrews 13:2)

**(I)** *Step Six*—Write out the *key thought* for each major division, remembering that the key thought is your stating the main idea in one sentence. Then write a key thought for the whole study. This becomes the "big idea" or theme of the study. In the process, you narrow down the material (as in a funnel) from the key thought of each verse to the key thought of the whole.

### HOSPITALITY—KEY THOUGHTS OF THE WHOLE STUDY

I. Hospitality defined:
   Being sensitive to the needs of people around me, including the stranger, and providing the necessary aid to meet those needs.
II. Hospitality demonstrated:
   By fulfilling the common courtesies in my culture so the guest knows he is welcome.
- A. An attitude of commitment and love for hospitality is essential.
- B. Time, effort, and provisions are part of the cost, but the benefits can be an unexpected heavenly guest.

*Key Thought for the Whole Study:* Hospitality is committing myself to others, including the stranger, and communicating a genuine interest in them by extending cultural courtesies and providing for their needs.

**(A)** *Step Seven*—Choose from the possible applications listed in your *Observations* the one on which God would have you work.

### HOSPITALITY—APPLICATION

I attend a large church where it is easy to become lost among the people. I don't go out of my way to greet people I don't recognize. I merely go on my own way.

This is contrary to the Bible's teaching of having a life style of being hospitable.

I will try to greet those around me following the worship service, introduce myself, and inquire if they're visitors. I'll welcome them and ask if I can be of any service to them (such as, finding a Sunday School class).

### Advanced Topical Study

The following additional steps are optional and should only be tried after you have gained proficiency in the first part of the study. This cannot be overemphasized: don't try to tackle too much at once. Add to your methodology slowly. You are seeking to develop life-long habits of Bible study.

**(I)** *Step Eight*—Take the key thought of your study and write several paragraphs elaborating on the central truth. View this key thought as the pivotal point of your elaboration. Never stray far from it. The purpose here is to nail down the basic truths or principles found in the study.

## HOSPITALITY—ELABORATING ON THE KEY THOUGHT

Hospitality is committing myself to others, including the stranger, and communicating a genuine interest in them by extending cultural courtesies and providing for their needs.

Hospitality is a commitment in that it is not merely entertaining but a way of life—a lifestyle. Entertaining is something you choose to do or don't do depending on your will, but hospitality is an openness of life and home. It is giving of yourself to others in an attitude of commitment, not obligation.

Hospitality is communicating to your guest an interest in him by extending common courtesies in keeping with our culture. This might include a warm handshake, the offering of a beverage, time to converse (without mentally being preoccupied as you listen), and the invitation to a meal or lodging if it is appropriate to the time of day and circumstances.

The guest may have needs other than physical (such as, food and drink). These may include acceptance or a problem which needs to be discussed. Hospitality includes fellowship with genuine interest in seeking to minister to the needs of the other person.

Because hospitality involves giving, there is a cost involved. It could be in time, effort, or material things, yet the cost is only one aspect of hospitality. The other is the reward of hospitality. This may or may not be evident immediately. God is a giving God and when His children participate in His nature, He rewards them, sometimes with a "heavenly" guest.

Therefore, by committing myself to others, including the stranger, and communicating a genuine interest in them by extending cultural courtesies and providing for their needs, I am obeying the biblical admonition of being hospitable.

(C) *Step Nine*—Referring to the material found in Chapter 10, make a chart on your topical study. This will be a helpful step in viewing the study as a whole and seeing how the parts relate to one another. The type of topical study you have done will influence the kind of chart you select.

## HOSPITALITY — CHART

| BIBLICAL HOSPITALITY | CULTURAL ENTERTAINING |
|---|---|
| Reflection of a lifestyle | Fulfilling an obligation |
| Sharing what you have | Showing off what you have |
| Stranger is welcome | The well-known person is welcome |
| Home as a hospice | Home as an ivory tower |

Figure 10

(I) *Step Ten*—Refer to outside material on the topic you studied and add or alter any part of your study. This last step is a helpful "check" on your conclusions, especially if you plan on any public presentation of your study.

# 6 The Biographical Method of Bible Study

This is a "fun" kind of Bible study, for you have an opportunity to explore the characters of people the Holy Spirit has placed in the Bible and learn from their lives. Paul, writing to the Corinthians, said, "These things happened to them as examples and were written down as warnings for us, on whom the fulfillment of the ages has come" (1 Corinthians 10:11).

A great deal of material has been written on some of the people in the Bible. When you study people like Jesus, Abraham, and

Moses, you may want to narrow down your study to areas such as, "The life of Jesus as revealed in John's Gospel," "Moses during the Exodus," or "What the New Testament says about Abraham." Constantly work at keeping your Bible studies to manageable size.

The same reference materials suggested in Chapter 5 are useful here.

As in the Verse Analysis method, a letter indicating the part you are doing has been noted next to each of the steps to draw attention to the four basic parts of Bible study.

(O) OBSERVATION
(I) INTERPRETATION
(C) CORRELATION
(A) APPLICATION

## Basic Biographical Study

For the purpose of illustration, we will use Rahab in this study.

(C) *Step One*—Choose the person you want to study and set the boundaries of the study (for example, "The life of David before he became king"). Using a concordance or cyclopedic index, locate the references that have to do with the person you are studying. Read these several times, and write a summary for each.

### RAHAB—REFERENCES

Joshua    2:1—a harlot living in Jericho
          2:3—the king of Jericho asks about the spies from her
          2:4—she hid the spies and lied to the king
          2:5—she purposely distracted the men of the city
          2:6—she hid the spies under flax
          2:8-9—she acknowledged that the Lord had conquered Jericho

          2:10—the rumor of the Exodus and victory over the
             Amorites

          2:11—the fear of her people and the fact that the
             Lord was God of all

          2:12-13—she asked for safety for herself and her
             family

          2:14—the spies make her a promise

          2:15—she provided their escape route

          2:16—she gave them a plan for safety

          2:17-20—the spies plan for her safety

          2:21—the sign of her commitment

          6:22-23—Rahab's rescue along with her family

Matthew  1:5—Rahab's place in the genealogy of Jesus Christ

Hebrews  11:31—by faith she didn't die because she received
             the spies

James     2:25—she was justified by her action of sending the
             spies away

**(O)** *Step Two*—Take a sheet of paper and mark *OBSERVA-TIONS* on the top. Use this sheet throughout the study. Include on this page:

1. Observations—Note any and every detail you notice about this person. Who was he? What did he do? Where did he live? When did he live? Why did he do what he did? How did he accomplish it? Note details about him and his character.

2. Problems—Write out what you don't understand about this person and events in his life.

3. Possible application—Mark several of these during the course of your study, and write an **(A)** in the margin. At the conclusion of your study, you will return to these possible applications and select the one on which the Holy Spirit will have you focus.

(No illustration is included here, for the process is the same as *Step Two* under the *Topical Method of Bible Study,* pages 55-59.)

(O) *Step Three*—In paragraph form, write a brief sketch of the person's life. Include the important events and characteristics stating the facts without interpretation. Keep the material as chronological as possible.


RAHAB—A SKETCH OF HER LIFE

Rahab was a harlot in the town of Jericho, which was situated across the Jordan River in the land of Canaan. She, along with other members of her community, had heard how God had allowed the Israelites to cross the Red Sea on dry land and how they had also defeated the two kings of the Amorites.

When the spies came to her door she received them in peace and hid them from the king of Jericho, who was seeking their lives. She lied to the king that they were not there and sent the men of the city on a false chase after them.

She requested of the spies safety for herself and her family testifying to them that she believed the Israelite God to be the God of heaven and earth based on what she had heard of His acts.

The spies promised her safety if she wouldn't reveal their whereabouts and have all her family in her house when they conquered Jericho. Proof of their mutual commitment was a scarlet cord hanging from her window.

Her life was spared at the fall of Jericho and later she is found as the great great grandmother of King David and thus in the lineage of Jesus Christ.

The New Testament also records her faith and justification by her act of receiving the spies.


(I) *Step Four*—List the strengths and weaknesses of the person. Why did God consider him/her great? When did he or she fall short?

## RAHAB—STRENGTHS AND WEAKNESSES

*Strengths:* Based on very little knowledge (a rumor), Rahab staked her whole life and the lives of her family on what she heard. She *applied* what she knew. God considers this greatness—to believe Him and act on what you have. Her people had the same information, yet they didn't believe.

*Weaknesses:* She was a liar and a traitor to her country.

**(I)** *Step Five*—Choose the key verse for his/her life. This is the verse or passage that more than any other sums up the direction of that person's life. State the crowning achievement or contribution of that life.

## RAHAB—KEY VERSE

"By faith the prostitute Rahab because she welcomed the spies, was not killed with those who were disobedient" (Hebrews 11:31).

Her faith was exercised while she was a prostitute and God counts her great at that stage of her life, not following her acceptance into the Jewish community. She acted on the little knowledge she had by hiding the spies and believed that Jehovah was the true God of heaven and earth.

**(I)** *Step Six*—In one sentence, state the key thought regarding the person's life. This may be positive or negative. Here you are trying to sum up the person's life in one sentence. There should be a correlation between this key thought and the key verse in *Step Five*.

## RAHAB—KEY THOUGHT

Rahab was willing to take great risks with God on the basis of little information, and God considered this true greatness.

**(A)** *Step Seven*—Choose from the possible applications listed in your *Observations* the one on which God would have you work.

RAHAB—APPLICATION

It is easy to fall into the habit of reading the Bible to gain new insights and miss the life-changing aspects of application. I am guilty of this.

Since the key to a changed life is applying the Word of God to my life, not increasing my knowledge, I will pray and commit myself to apply a truth of Scripture each time I read the Bible.

## Advanced Biographical Study

The following steps may be added if and when you feel they will help in your biographical studies. They are optional and should only be included progressively as you gain confidence and proficiency.

(O) *Step Eight*—Trace the historical background of the person. Use a Bible dictionary to augment this step only when necessary. The following questions should stimulate your thinking.

1. When did the person live? What were the political, social, religious, and economic conditions of his time?
2. Where was the person born? Who were his parents? Was there anything unusual surrounding his birth and childhood?
3. What was his vocation? Was he a teacher, farmer, or in some other occupation? Did this influence his later ministry? How?
4. Who was his spouse? Did they have any children? What were they like? Did they help or hinder his life and ministry?
5. Chart the person's travels. Where did he/she go? Why? What was accomplished?
6. How did the person die? Was there anything extraordinary in his life?

### RAHAB—HISTORICAL BACKGROUND

Jericho, the City of Palms, was in the land of Canaan. It was on a caravan route between Egypt to the south and Babylon to the north. Canaan consisted of small kingdoms, each with fortified cities and a king (see Joshua 9:1-2). Jericho was fortified with a double wall, and Rahab's house was on that wall.

The Canaanites were the descendants of Ham (see Genesis 19:18-25), and their worship consisted of idolatry, fertility rites, and human sacrifices to Baal.

From the time the residents of Jericho heard of the Exodus, they lived in fear. The men of the city had hearts that "melted" within them.

According to the Bible account, the flax had been harvested since it was on the roof to dry, thereby setting the story in the end of March or first of April.

Later Rahab married Salmon and had a son, Boaz. Boaz married the Gentile Ruth, after whom the Old Testament book is named. Their son Obed bore Jesse, who was the father of Israel's greatest king, David.

**(I)** *Step Nine*—Write a couple of paragraphs on the person's philosophy of life. What motivated him or her? What were his or her attitudes? What were his or her life objectives? What did the person want out of life and did he or she get it?

### RAHAB—PHILOSOPHY OF LIFE

Rahab's philosophy of life was to believe that the God of the Israelites must be the true and living God. She had heard of the miracles He had performed for His people. While her countrymen lived in fear, she lived in faith, believing that God had already conquered Jericho. Her faith motivated her to receive the spies, hide them, and help them escape. She also wanted safety for herself and her family, which she received. She acquired a permanent place in the history of Israel and in the lineage of Jesus Christ.

**(C)** *Step Ten*—Referring to the material in Chapter 10, make a chart on this person. Make it chronological, marking the various phases of his or her life. If you desire, make another chart showing his or her relationship to others who entered his or her life. Figure 11 is an illustration of the life of Rahab in chart form.

## RAHAB - CHART

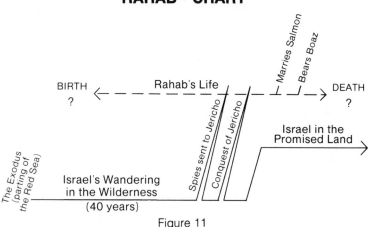

Figure 11

**(C)** *Step Eleven*—Compare and/or contrast the person with others in the Bible. The person compared may be a contemporary, or if it is someone like Moses or Abraham, the comparison may be made with Christ.

### RAHAB—COMPARISON

An interesting comparison to Rahab is Lot's wife. She had a family relationship with Abraham and was aware of God's promises to him. Yet when the angels came to deliver her from the destruction of Sodom and gave specific commands not to look back, she didn't believe. This unbelief resulted in her judgment as she turned into a pillar of salt.

Chapters 8–11 have been added to further stimulate your mind in expanding your biographical study and making it an even greater challenge to you. Just as it isn't necessary to include all of the above eleven steps in your study, so also don't feel that you need to incorporate all the suggestions in Chapters 8–11. They simply give you an opportunity to create your own personal study from a variety of ideas. Experiment till the method maximizes your ability to glean from your Bible study what you want.

# SECTION 11 Improving Your Bible Study Skills

# 7 Improvement Is for Everyone

Section II will help you improve the skills that you have already learned and launch you into developing your own methods of doing Bible study. Before you use the methods suggested here, however, make sure you are familiar with the methods described in Section I of this book. After you have done the Bible studies described there for some time, using those methods, refer to this part.

The contents of this section will help you go into greater depth into the four major essentials or parts of Bible study—observation, interpretation, correlation, and application. As you begin to sense the need for some additional help in a particular part of your Bible study, or want some new ideas, refer to the appropriate part.

This section will teach you new concepts of Bible study as well as new methods. Take sufficient time to understand any new concepts thoroughly. You will want to employ these in any of the methods you use, i.e., analytical, synthetic, topical, etc.

The suggestions in this section are only a sampling of the hundreds that are available. Use your own creativity to develop new methods, but before you do, take time to learn the methods presented. True creativity follows structure.

# 8 Observation: The Role of a Detective

---

| OBSERVATION |
| --- |
| **The recording of what may be seen in a selected method of Bible study.** |

*Webster's New Collegiate Dictionary* defines observation as the "act of recognizing and noting a fact or occurrence"; it means to be mentally aware of what one sees. The purpose of observation in Bible study is to saturate yourself with the content of the passage of Scripture, to become as familiar as possible with all that the biblical writer is saying and implying.

Accuracy is important in observation. Not everything you read will be of equal value in ascertaining the meaning of the passage. So you will have to learn to discern what is important and what is not. Practice and concentration are the two ingredients that will sharpen your expertise.

Jesus' last words of instruction to His disciples were to prepare them for the time when He would no longer be physically with them. He assured them that "the Counselor, the Holy Spirit, whom the Father will send in my name, will *teach* you all things and will remind you of everything I have said to you" (John 14:26). A little later on in the same conversation He said, "But when He, the Spirit of truth, comes, He will *guide* you into all truth" (John 16:13).

A prayerful dependence on the Holy Spirit is key to all aspects of Bible study, and especially to observation. Diligence, openness, dependence, an eagerness to learn—all these must characterize the student as he begins digging in the Word.

How do you begin observing? Where do you start? Take a piece of paper (8½'' x 11'' will do fine) and begin to record all you see. No item or idea is insignificant. Write it down so your mind can free itself to look for new things. The following suggestions are not necessarily given in the order of their importance. You will want to pick and choose from them depending on your level of proficiency and the type of material you are studying. Some suggestions will be more applicable to a character study, for example, than to an analytic study.

## Have the Right Mental Attitude

You have already learned that a basic requirement for making good observations is a prayerful dependence on the Holy Spirit. As you have worked on making good observations, you have probably become aware that more is required than just that attitude. Five more requirements are necessary as well.

1. *Observation requires an act of the will.* You must have the will and the desire to be aware of what is in the biblical text, then to perceive and recognize what is there. You must have the determination to know and to learn. For example, when you meet people for the first time, do you remember their names? If not, it is likely that you have not purposed in your mind that you are going to learn their names. Learning begins with an act of the will—you must want to learn.

2. *Observation requires a persistence to know.* Learning is never easy. It requires diligence and discipline. You cannot have an effective disciple without him or her being a disciplined person. One of the keys in persisting in your personal Bible study is to see that the results are really worth the effort and the work that you have put into it. Take time to reflect on the results that have taken place in your life over the past six months because you have been doing Bible study faithfully.

3. *Observation requires patience.* In a day when you have instant communication, instant everything, there is a tendency to want an instant education. True learning, however, takes a great deal of time. You cannot take shortcuts in the learning process. The so-called short cuts are in fact only short circuits; they lead to ineffective results. In personal Bible study as well as in everything else in the Christian life, the process is as important as the product.

4. *Observation requires diligent recording.* As you look over the observations you recorded in some of your previous Bible studies, you will probably notice that there are some that you have completely forgotten. You will remember only a small portion of the observations you had made. So it is best for you to record all the observations you make in your personal Bible study diligently. In doing so, you will again see the importance and value of having a study Bible where you can keep a record of your good observations for the next time you study that portion of Scripture.

5. *Observation requires caution.* Observation is only the first step in studying the Bible—interpretation, correlation, and application must follow. Three warnings must be heeded.

    a. Don't lose yourself in the details; divide your time proportionately for all parts of the passage under study.

    b. Don't stop with observations, but go on to ask questions and seek meaningful answers.

    c. Don't give equal weight to everything; carefully discern what is more important.

## Use the Six Basic Questions

1. *WHO?* List all the people involved. In 1 Thessalonians 1 you will note that Paul talks about *we, you,* and *they.* In verse 1 the *we* included Paul, Silas, and Timothy. The same verse also suggests that *you* refers to the believers in the city of Thessalonica. Verse 7 reveals who is included in the *they*—those in the provinces of Macedonia and Achaia.

2. *WHAT?* What happened? What ideas are expressed? What are the results? In 1 Thessalonians 1 Paul is discussing the effects of the gospel. The Thessalonians' labor was not in vain: lives were changed (verse 5). The Thessalonian believers assumed responsibility for sharing the Good News with others (verse 8). Paul could see from his "spiritual grandchildren" the results of his ministry to the Thessalonians (verses 9-10).

3. *WHERE?* Where does this take place? What is the geographical setting? Here a good Bible dictionary will prove helpful: Zondervan's *Pictorial Dictionary of the Bible* is a good investment if you don't already own a similar volume. As you investigate the background of this city, you discover that it was rebuilt and given its name in 315 B.C. at the time of Alexander the Great. It was named after Alexander's step-sister. Located in the northeastern corner of the Thermaic Gulf (here you will want to consult your maps), it straddled the Egnation Way, a famous road in Macedonia used by the Romans. The city had the best natural harbor in Macedonia. During Paul's time it was the capital of that province. Many additional similar observations could be made.

4. *WHEN?* When did this take place? What was the historical background? Consulting your Bible dictionary once again, you discover that Paul founded the church in Thessalonica on his second missionary journey (see Acts 17:1-9). After ministering in this city, Paul and his team worked their way south through the Greek provinces of Macedonia and Achaia ending up in Corinth. It was from that city that Paul wrote 1 Thessalonians in about A.D. 54.

5. *WHY?* Why did this happen? What is the purpose or stated reason? Continuing to use 1 Thessalonians as our example, we find by reading the historical account of Paul's second journey (Acts 17–18) that he was plagued by a group of unbelieving Jews. These men followed Paul from city to city causing trouble. Persecutions of the new Christians inevitably followed. Timothy was sent back to Thessalonica to see how the believers fared and to encourage them in their Christian lives. Timothy returned with a positive report and Paul followed up with this letter. His purpose in writing was to communicate his confidence in them, assure them of the hope of the resurrection (a particularly precious doctrine during times of persecution), and exhort them to holy living.

6. *HOW?* How are things accomplished? How well? How quickly? By what method? Paul followed up his ministry to the Thessalonians by sending Timothy back to see them and then writing this letter. Though Paul had ministered there but a short time, the Thessalonian believers had become committed disciples of Christ.

## Discover the Form or Structure of the Passage Under Study

As you observe the contents of a passage you are studying, you will also want to become aware of the form it takes. How God says something is as important as what He says. You should ask yourself questions like, *How does the writer deal with the content? What form or structure does he use?* Some examples you may notice are:

- The writer asks four questions and answers them.
- The writer lists seventeen things we are to avoid.
- The writer gives us five commands we are to obey.
- The writer makes three declarative statements and then supports them.

The writer of a section of Scripture may place his content in the form of poetry, narrative, parable, logical argument, discourse, practical advice, history, drama, or some other forms. The way that the content of God's Word unfolds reveals the mind and method of the writer in communicating God's truth, and gives you further insight and feeling into the meaning of the passage under study. Some other things to look for as you examine structure are:

- Use of cause and effect (as in 1 Thessalonians 1)
- The movement from particulars to generalities (as in 1 Thessalonians 2), or from generalities to particulars (as in 1 Thessalonians 5)
- Use of Old Testament references in the New Testament (as in Romans 10)
- Use of illustrations in the text of the main argument or narrative (as in Galatians 4)
- Use of the current events of the times (as in Luke 13:1-5)

Some of the methods writers employ to relate their messages are:

1. *Relating the way things are*—1 Thessalonians 1 is a good example of this. Paul is communicating certain truths in this passage, but he does that by reviewing a sequence of events they all had in common. We might paraphrase this chapter as follows: "I came to you, preached the gospel, and you responded. This response manifested itself in your sharing the gospel with those near you. Their response to the gospel assured me that you were serious in your commitment to Christ."

2. *Admonition or exhortation*—Paul's letter to the Galatians illustrates this. The Galatians had bought the message of the Judaizers. Paul exhorts them to consider the implications of following what he considers grievous error. In Galatians 2:1-14 Paul relates *the way things are* as he does in 1 Thessalonians 1, but this is parenthetical and illustrative of the main argument he is setting forth. Commands to obey and errors to avoid are the kinds of things to look for in this type of passage.

3. *Teaching*—Jesus' dissertation commonly referred to as the Sermon on the Mount (Matthew 5–7), and Paul's Epistle to the Romans are examples of the teaching style of communication. The

message is timeless in that the author is not addressing a current situation as Paul does in his letter to the Galatians. In Romans, Paul uses a common technique of teaching: asking questions and then answering them. For example, he asks the question, ''What advantage, then, is there in being a Jew, or what value is there in circumcision?'' (Romans 3:1). Then he proceeds to answer his own questions, much like a catechism.

4. *Parables*—These are frequently used by Jesus as a poignant way of driving home spiritual truth. With parables, the student seeks to discover the main point being made and must be careful not to allow his imagination to carry him to conclusions not intended by the story. Particularly with parables, it is possible to observe too much.

5. *Narrative*—Large portions of the Bible take this form of writing. Genesis, Exodus, most of Numbers, Joshua through Esther, most of the Gospels and Acts are all narrative in form.

6. *Other methods*—Practical advice is found in Proverbs and various poetic styles in the Psalms, other poetical books, and many of the prophetical books. As you begin your study, note the form or structure carefully, for it will greatly assist you in identifying the means used by the writer in communicating his message.

## Find the Key Words

In some passages that you study, the key word jumps out at you and is readily apparent. *Love* in 1 Corinthians 13 and *faith* in Hebrews 11 are examples of this. Most of the time, however, it requires diligent work to discover the key words in a passage.

While Webster's dictionary is helpful in defining the English words of a Bible passage, it is inadequate in giving the literal meanings of Hebrew or Greek words or phrases. To check the definition of a biblical word, the average person must rely on other resources. Often a Bible dictionary will give a more thorough and comprehensive description of a word or topic.

Other background material which will prove helpful in defining

New Testament words are W. E. Vine's *An Expository Dictionary of New Testament Words* and M. R. Vincent's *Word Studies in the New Testament. Girdlestone's Old Testament Synonyms* is a good reference for Old Testament word studies. Good commentaries, explaining the literal meaning of biblical words and phrases, will also be helpful. Without a command of either the Hebrew or Greek languages, you can profit in your study of the Scriptures from the excellent scholarship and research available in a few well chosen books.

Let us take 1 Peter 1 as our example. In the *King James Version,* Peter says, "that the trial of your faith" (verse 7). As you compare the word *trial* with the *Revised Standard Version,* you note that it is replaced with the word *genuineness.* The *New International Version* uses the phrase *proved genuine.* James Strong's *Exhaustive Concordance of the Bible* will give you the Greek word and the other places in the Bible where that same Greek word is used: Luke 14:19; 1 Corinthians 3:13; 2 Corinthians 8:22; 1 Thessalonians 2:4; and James 1:3, 12. And you find the word is used in a variety of ways.

Tracing the meaning of this Greek word *dokimos,* you find it means, "A test, the means of proof, the result of the contact of faith with trial, and hence the verification of faith" (Vincent's *Word Studies*). This is a key idea, not only in 1 Peter 1, but in the whole of his first epistle. These dispersed Christians were suffering for their faith. The difficulties were not without benefit, however. They revealed that their faith in Christ was genuine. Like gold purified by fire, the suffering Christian is "tested in battle and found to be pure and reliable." *Suffering* is one of the major themes in 1 Peter and *trial* (KJV) is a key word in understanding that suffering.

In Romans 3 words like *propitiation, justified, remission, redemption, righteousness,* and *forbearance* (KJV) are all key in understanding the meaning of this passage.

If you feel that your level of understanding of words such as these is small, and that such study is, at best, difficult, don't feel as though you are alone. These illustrations are meant to be suggestive of how you can go about studying a passage. Use what you feel comfortable with and leave the rest. At a later time when you feel comfortable with the tools you are using in your study, you will be ready to go back and add a few more.

### Consider Comparisons and Contrasts

Two kinds of observations to make in your personal Bible study are comparisons and contrasts. Comparisons show how things are alike; contrasts show how things are different. Make a special effort to find contrasts and comparisons in the passage you are studying. If there are none in that passage, try to find other Scriptures which will give you contrasts and comparisons with the section you are studying.

To help you in making observations of comparison and contrast, look for words like "even so," "as . . . so . . .," and "likewise." These are not the *only* words that provide comparisons, but they almost always do so. When you find a comparison, spend sufficient time thinking through the things being compared. Then record as many ways as possible in which they are alike.

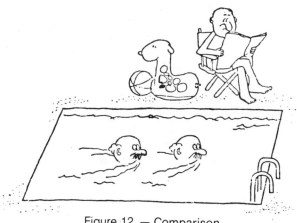

Figure 12 — Comparison

Contrasts may be more difficult to find because the range of intensity can vary from distinct contrasts to mild differences. Look for things which are similar in one respect and dissimilar in another. Key words to look for are "but," "nor," and "not."

Figure 13 — Contrast

In this observation exercise you will especially want to use cross-references. As you read a story or statement in the Scriptures, consider things which are similar in certain respects but different in others. Observing these contrasts will help you discern the overall truth of the Word of God.

In his letter to the Thessalonians, Paul makes two comparisons between his ministry and the role of parents with children. He compares his activities among them as being that of "a mother caring for her little children" (1 Thessalonians 2:7), and that he dealt with them "as a father deals with his own children" (2:11). Considering the characteristics of a mother, you might think about infant care, tenderness, caring for babies individually, and feeding them on schedule. Considering the role of the father, you would think of discipline, concern, instruction, and giving direction. Making these observations will give you additional insight into Paul's character and his relationship to the Thessalonians.

OBSERVATION: THE ROLE OF A DETECTIVE 89

Several contrasts also appear in this letter. Paul stated, for example, that his preaching was "not trying to please men *but* God" (2:4). Later, as he was exhorting them, he said, "Let us not be like others who are asleep, *but* let us be alert and self-controlled" (5:6).

The Book of Hebrews frequently makes use of comparisons and contrasts. Figure 14 is a chart made from such a treatment of Christ and Aaron in Hebrews 7.

## CONTRASTS BETWEEN THE TWO PRIESTHOODS
### (Hebrews 7)

| Chapter Divisions | MELCHIZEDEK/CHRIST | Contrasts in Verses | LEVI/AARON |
|---|---|---|---|
| 7:1-3 | WHO MELCHIZEDEK WAS | | |
| 7:4-10 | RECEIVED TITHES FROM ABRAHAM | 4 | PAID TITHES TO MELCHIZEDEK THROUGH ABRAHAM |
| | GAVE A BLESSING | 6 | RECEIVED A BLESSING |
| | LIVES FOREVER | 8 | DIED |
| 7:11-19 | FREE FROM AN IMPERFECT LAW | 11 | MARRIED TO AN IMPERFECT LAW |
| | PRIESTHOOD UNCHANGED BY VIRTUE OF HIS LIFE | 12/16 | PRIESTHOOD CHANGED BY VIRTUE OF HIS TRIBAL HERITAGE |
| | COULD MAKE PEOPLE PERFECT | 19 | COULD NOT MAKE PEOPLE PERFECT |
| 7:20-22 | WITH AN OATH | 20 | WITHOUT AN OATH |
| 7:23-25 | ONE PRIEST | 23/24 | MANY PRIESTS |
| | EVER LIVETH | 23/24 | DEATH |
| | ABLE TO SAVE | 25 | UNABLE TO SAVE |
| 7:26-28 | SEPARATE FROM SIN | 26/27 | SINNER |
| | OFFERED HIMSELF ONCE | 27 | OFFERED SACRIFICES (animals) MANY TIMES |
| | PERFECT | 28 | WEAK |
| | GOD/MAN | 28 | MAN |

Figure 14

**Investigate the Use of Old Testament References**

The only Scriptures people had in the early days of the church were the writings of the Old Testament. The advent of Jesus Christ was the fulfillment of what the Old Testament had promised. Because of this fact, New Testament writers constantly dip back into the Old Testament to show how Jesus is the Messiah or to relate the implications of this fact to the lives of people.

The Book of Galatians is a beautiful example of this. Paul, reasoning from the Old Testament, convinced those in the province of Galatia that Jesus was the Christ. Then the Judaizers followed his ministry, arguing from the same Old Testament that people coming to Christ had to follow Old Testament laws, such as circumcision, in order to be saved. In his letter, Paul argues back that the Old Testament itself teaches that these laws that the Judaizers were pressing should no longer be kept. Paul's selection and use of Old Testament references is absolutely masterful in proving this difficult point.

**Note the Progression of an Idea or Thought Chain**

Thought chains graphically associate similar ideas. You will need a study Bible you can mark and some colored pencils. Look through a passage for similar thoughts. Then using one color for similar ideas, draw a circle around each one. Using the same color, connect the circles with thin lines and give the chain a title. Use different colors to make other chains of associated thoughts.

Now consider chain titles to see how they fit together to make one theme of the passage. In Figure 15 only one chain has been worked out. It is the "Character of the Minister." Other chains might be titled "Effect of the Ministry" and "Concern for Young Christians." These lead to the theme, "How to Minister to Young Believers."

**1 THESSALONIANS 2:1**

*Paul's Ministry in Thessalonica*

2 You know, brothers, that our visit to you was not a failure. ²We had previously suffered and been insulted in Philippi, as you know, but with the help of our God (we dared) to tell you his gospel in spite of strong opposition. ³For the appeal we make does not spring from error or impure motives, nor are we trying to trick you. ⁴On the contrary, we speak as men (approved by God) to be entrusted with the gospel. We are not trying to please men but God, who tests our hearts. ⁵You know (we never used flattery), nor did we put on a mask to cover up greed—God is our witness. ⁶(We were not looking for praise from men), not from you or anyone else.

⁷As apostles of Christ we could have been a burden to you, but (we were gentle) among you, like a mother caring for her little children. ⁸(We loved you) so much that we were delighted to share with you not only the gospel of God but our lives as well, because you had become so dear to us. ⁹Surely you remember, brothers, our toil and hardship; we worked night and day in order not to be a burden to anyone while we preached the gospel of God to you.

¹⁰You are witnesses, and so is God, of (how holy, righteous and blameless we were among you) who believed. ¹¹For you know that we dealt with each of you as a father deals with his own children, ¹²encouraging, comforting and urging you to live lives worthy of God, who calls you into his kingdom and glory.

Figure 15

In 2 Timothy 1, Paul talks about not being ashamed of the gospel. Note his progression of thought:

- Verse 8—"Do not be ashamed . . ."
- Verse 12—"I am not ashamed . . ."
- Verse 16—"Onesiphorus . . . was not ashamed . . ."

A more technical illustration of this may be seen in the idea of *imputation* used by Paul in the Book of Romans:

- Romans 3:21-31—the imputation of Christ's righteousness to the sinner
- Romans 4—imputation illustrated in the life of Abraham
- Romans 5:12-21—the imputation of Adam's sin to mankind
- Romans 6–8—the outworking of imputation in the life of the believer

## Be Alert for Proportions

The law of proportions is one of the keys to maintaining a balance of emphasis in your personal Bible study. Make sure that you are observing such proportions as importance of the subject, people involved, the time element, and the subject matter itself. The following chart of the Book of Acts will help you observe the time element as it is found in the book.

| Chapters | 1 | 2 | 3-8 | 9-12 | 13-14 | 15 | 16:1-18:22 | 18:23-21:16 | 21:17-28:31 |
|---|---|---|---|---|---|---|---|---|---|
| Time Span | 50 days | 1 day | 2 years | 9 years | 1½ years | few days | 2½ years | 4 years | 5 years |

Figure 16

Observe also how much of Paul's first letter to the Thessalonians deals with the second coming of Jesus Christ. The topic is mentioned in each chapter and discussed at length toward the end of the letter (see 1 Thessalonians 1:10; 2:19; 3:13; 4:13-18; 5:1-11). Also notice the references Paul made to his unblamable conduct and behavior before the people in Thessalonica. These proportion observations can give you a clue to Paul's major emphases in writing that first epistle.

## Record Repetitions

As you do your Bible study, take particular note of the repetition of words, phrases, and expressions in the passage being studied. You can do this by making a chart of the repetitions in the passage. The benefit of this method is not in filling out the chart, but in enabling you to ask the right questions after you have seen the repetitions in the passage. An example from 1 Thessalonians 3 may be seen below in Figure 17.

| WORD OR PHRASE | NUMBER OF REPETITIONS | VERSES USED |
|---|---|---|
| FAITH | 5 | 2, 5, 6, 7, 10 |
| AFFLICTION | 3 | 3, 4, 7 |

Figure 17

Observing that the word *faith* appears five times in this section, you might ask, ''Why is faith mentioned so often?'' Seeing the repetition of the word *affliction,* you might conclude that faith is increased by the right response to affliction.

In almost every passage you will study, there will be words or phrases that will be repeated. Look for them and examine them carefully. Determine why they are repeated and how they are related.

Observation also includes the opposite aspect of repetition—omission. As you study a given passage, think to yourself, *What words or phrases would I have included in writing this?* Then continue your observation by asking questions like, ''If these thoughts and ideas are omitted, why are they omitted?'' ''Is there a substitute the author used?'' ''What is that substitute?'' Obviously, it is much more difficult to observe omissions than to see repetitions, but omissions must be carefully noted.

For example, a notable omission in the Book of Acts is the complete absence of the word *love.* On the other hand, the results of love, unity and oneness, are mentioned often.

## Visualize the Verbs

Another key to making good observations is discerning the action or movement of a passage. In grammar, action is carried by verbs. They tell us what is being done, and reveal the movement or flow of a passage.

Underline all the verbs in the passage you are studying, then list them on your Bible study worksheet. After you have underlined them all, examine them carefully. What kind of action do the verbs portray? Are most of them active or passive? Does the subject influence the action or is it being acted on? Do the verbs indicate that the passage is basically a narrative or poetry? Are there any quotations? Are the verbs imperatives—do they give commands? Which verbs are repeated? What is the significance of their usages?

For example, in Hebrews 11 the verbs are active, indicating that the believer has a vital role in the life of faith. He must respond to what God is doing in his life.

In Ephesians 1:3-14 the verbs are passive and indicate that the believer is acted on. Observing the use of verbs in this passage gives us the clue that the emphasis is on what is done for the believer rather than what he does or must do.

The following illustration from 1 Thessalonians 1 shows the underlining process (Fig. 18).

## Picture the Illustrations

Have you ever been struck by how many verbal illustrations there are in the Bible? Many of the writers God used to record His Word talked in pictures. Jesus used this device often as He called His followers vines, sheep, fishers of men, farmers, and many other such expressions.

As you study, pay particular attention to finding illustrations being used by the writer of the passage you are observing. Some illustrations are obvious, like the vine and the branches in John 15. Others are not so obvious, but Scripture abounds in illustrations

# 1 Thessalonians

**1** Paul, Silas[a] and Timothy,

To the church of the Thessalonians, who are in God the Father and the Lord Jesus Christ:

Grace and peace to you.

### Thanksgiving for the Thessalonians' Faith

[2]We always <u>thank</u> God for all of you, <u>mentioning</u> you in our prayers. [3]We continually <u>remember</u> before our God and Father your work produced by faith, your labor <u>prompted</u> by love, and your endurance <u>inspired</u> by hope in our Lord Jesus Christ.

[4]Brothers <u>loved</u> by God, we <u>know</u> that he has <u>chosen</u> you, [5]because our gospel <u>came</u> to you not simply with words, but also with power, <u>with</u> the Holy Spirit and with deep conviction. You <u>know</u> how we <u>lived</u> among you for your sake. [6]You <u>became</u> imitators of us and of the Lord; in spite of severe suffering, you <u>welcomed</u> the message with the joy <u>given</u> by the Holy Spirit. [7]And so you <u>became</u> a model to all the believers in Macedonia and Achaia. [8]The Lord's message <u>rang out</u> from you not only in Macedonia and Achaia—your faith in God <u>has become known</u> everywhere. Therefore we do not need <u>to say</u> anything about it, [9]for they themselves <u>report</u> what kind of reception you <u>gave us.</u> They <u>tell</u> how you <u>turned</u> to God from idols <u>to serve</u> the living and true God, [10]and <u>to wait</u> for his Son from heaven, whom he <u>raised</u> from the dead—Jesus, who <u>rescues</u> us from the coming wrath.

Figure 18

and word pictures. In James 3 alone, there are at least nine different illustrations (and comparisons and contrasts).

Once you observe an illustration, think through on how it clarifies the subject of the passage. Try to think of other illustrations that Scripture uses to present this subject. Then compare and contrast your illustration with these. For example, Paul's use of a thief in the night illustrates the need for being prepared (1 Thessalonians 5:2); a woman with child illustrates suddenness (5:3); and a breastplate of faith illustrates being equipped (5:8).

If there are no illustrations in the passage you are studying, which is highly unlikely, then look for illustrations and examples in other portions of Scripture relevant to the passage under study.

### Examine the Explanations

An explanation is anything that is used to illustrate, clarify, illuminate, describe, or demonstrate. An explanation may be one verse long or a whole chapter.

To understand an explanation clearly, you must follow the logic of the writer. What point is he trying to make? How is he trying to make it? How does he present it?

Sometimes the Scriptures explain a question that is not stated but implied. Often a statement in one verse will cause you to ask a question, and the following verse will then answer your question. Be sure to note this kind of tie-in between verses and paragraphs.

For example, Paul said, "We maintain that a man is justified by faith apart from observing the law" (Romans 3:28). A natural question which may come out of observation on this statement might be, "Could people in the Old Testament be saved?"

In the next two paragraphs (Romans 4:1-8), Paul explains how Abraham and David were both justified by faith without the deeds of the law. This helps explain the earlier statement, but don't presume that the paragraphs of Romans 4 were written primarily to explain your question on Romans 3:28.

## Be Sensitive to Connecting Words and Conjunctions

Someone once said that the little two-letter word *if* connotes the difference between law and grace. It certainly connotes condition, and when speaking of what God wants to do in the lives of people is an immediate indication of whether the people's response will affect what God promises to do. For example, God said to the nation of Israel, "Now if you obey me fully and keep my covenant, then out of all nations you will be my treasured possession" (Exodus 19:5). This did not come about because Israel did not obey.

Other important connectives include *therefore,* which introduces a summary of ideas or the results of some action; *because, or, for,* and *then* are words that often introduce a reason or result; *but* lets you know there is a contrast that follows; and *in order that* is a phrase often used to set forth a purpose. Stay alert for these in your study.

## Be Willing to Change Your Viewpoint

In order to change your viewpoint, you will have to eliminate preconceived ideas. Do not allow these to control or even color your thinking about the Word of God. Read your study passage as though you were an impartial observer. In his first letter to the Thessalonians, Paul levels several accusations at a particular group of people (1 Thessalonians 2:14-16). At first glance, out of some preconceived ideas you might have, you might envision these people as being vicious and cruel. But the fact is that this group was well respected and well thought of in their society. With this in mind, you may need to change your viewpoint and reread this passage making new observations.

One of the more interesting ways to change your viewpoint is to put yourself in another person's shoes. How would you feel if you were the author of this epistle? (When Paul wrote Ephesians, he was in prison.) How would you as a recipient understand the message? (Paul rebukes his recipients in 1 Corinthians.) What would a third party at the scene think of the situation as he listened to Paul? (Silas and Timothy were with Paul when he wrote 1 Thessalonians.) What would strict Jews think of Paul's letter to the Galatians? Or strict Romans of James' letter? You need to learn to observe from different perspectives.

## Mark Your Bible as You Read

You should have a study Bible with wide margins that you can use to record your observations. (Many are available on the market today—check with your local bookstore or the American Bible Society.) As you make observations on a passage you have chosen to study, mark it in the text and in the margins. You may use some or all of the following devices: brackets, parallel diagonal lines in the margin, circles, vertical lines in the margins, arrows, inked in words and/or phrases, marked through words and/or phrases, underlining (see the section *Visualizing the Verbs* earlier in the chapter). Also you may create your own symbols, marks, and system.

In marking a study Bible (not a good reading Bible made of India paper) you can use pen and ink, ballpoint, and fine and course felt-tip pens. To mark *through* words and phrases for emphasis use a light highlighter felt-tip pen to allow you to read the words through it. Use india ink in marking a fine Bible. Some examples follow in a marked-up copy of 1 Thessalonians 2:1-12. (Fig. 19.)

## Summary

Do not become discouraged if your observations do not immediately bear the fruit you desire. It is hard work and, like any other skill, takes time to develop. Nor should you feel like a failure if you are unable to apply all these suggestions to your Bible study. They have been given to serve as a set of "handles" for you to get a grip on *observation*. Some of these "handles" won't apply to every passage.

1 THESSALONIANS 2:1

*Paul's Ministry in Thessalonica*

2 You <u>know</u>, brothers, that our visit to you was not a failure. We had previously suffered and been insulted in Philippi, as you know, but with the help of our God we dared to tell you <u>his gospel</u> in spite of strong opposition. ³For the appeal we make does not spring from error or impure motives, nor are we trying to trick you. ⁴On the contrary, we speak as men approved by God to be entrusted with <u>the</u> gospel. We are not trying to please men but God, who tests <u>our hearts</u>. ⁵You know we never used flattery, nor did we put on a mask to cover up greed—God is our witness. ⁶We were not looking for praise from men, not from you or anyone else.

⁷As apostles of Christ we could have been a burden to you, but we were gentle among you, like a mother caring for her little children. ⁸We loved you so much that we were delighted to share with you not only the <u>gospel of God</u> but our lives as well, because you had become so dear to us. ⁹Surely you remember, brothers, our toil and hardship; we worked night and day in order not to be a burden to anyone while we preached the <u>gospel of God</u> to you.

¹⁰You are witnesses, and so is God, of how holy, righteous and blameless we were among you who believed. ¹¹For you know that we dealt with each of you as a father deals with his own children, ¹²encouraging, comforting and urging you to live lives worthy of God, who <u>calls</u> you into his kingdom and glory.

*[Handwritten margin notes: "See Acts 16", "Contrast", "←", "Key: Sharing our lives with others ←"]*

Figure 19

You will find prayerful reflection to be indispensable. Be imaginative. Put yourself in the role of the writer or the people you are studying. How did they respond? How should they have responded? Seek to feel things as they must have felt them. Dialogue with them.

Also, be patient. If, after your study, you find you have overlooked an important *observation*, remember that others never stop discovering new and fresh insights from passages with which they have lived for many years.

# Interpretation: The Role of a Decision Maker

| | |
|---|---|
| **INTERPRETATION** | Observation seeks to answer the question "What does it *say?*" Interpretation seeks to answer the question "What does it *mean?*" The dictionary defines interpretation as "The act or process of explaining; to clarify the meaning of; to offer an explanation." In this part of the Bible study, you are seeking to clarify the *meaning* of the |
| **Understanding the meaning of what has been observed in Bible study.** | |

passage and understand the writer's *meaning* as he communicated these words to the people of his day.

101

Foundational to this step in Bible study is the application of the 24 rules of interpretation stated in the book *A Layman's Guide to Interpreting the Bible*. They form the ground rules for understanding the Bible. You should review them periodically, for the value of your Bible study will be in direct proportion to their application.

Interpretation follows observation. It is analogous to drawing the net around a school of fish you have just caught. It is an exciting part of your Bible study, for it is a time in which you come to some conclusions. The individual insights that made up your observations are now brought together into a coherent whole.

The three parts to the interpretive process are purpose, key thought, and flow.

## Purpose

Here your objective is to determine why the writer is bringing up the subject. Paul, writing to the church at Rome, said, "For everything that was written in the past was written to teach us" (Romans 15:4). What the Holy Spirit has included in the Bible is there in order that we might learn from it. Determining the *purpose* of the book, passage, poem, story, or whatever else is the first step in interpretation.

As you do a synthetic study of Galatians, for example, you learn that Paul's purpose for writing that letter was to communicate that a person is justified by faith in Jesus Christ apart from the works of the law.

Sometimes the purpose is fairly easy to discover, as is the case with the Gospel of John. John states his purpose for writing: "These are written that you may believe that Jesus is the Christ [the Old Testament Messiah], the Son of God, and that by believing you may have life in his name" (John 20:31).

The purpose of the writer of Hebrews beginning with a comparison of Jesus Christ to angels (Chapters 1–2) is to establish the fact that God's revelation to man in the person of Christ is through no mere angel. Rather, He is the eternal Creator God of the universe.

In the Old Testament, when God wanted to speak authoritatively to His people, He frequently sent an angel. Jesus is infinitely better than the angels.

As you study the narration of an event, seek to discover its purpose. Why did Elijah retreat into the wilderness after his spectacular victory at Mount Carmel? (See 1 Kings 18–19.) Why did God keep Israel at Mount Sinai for such a long time after the Exodus? (See Exodus 19–40.) Similar questions should be asked in your study of Bible topics and biographies.

## Key Thought

The *key thought* is the "big idea," theme, or distilled essence of the book, passage, topic, or person you are studying. As much as possible, state the key thought in one sentence. Make it a complete sentence with a subject and predicate. Generally speaking, the longer and more complicated the theme, the less you understand what it is. A good rule of thumb is to try to limit your key thought to about 20-30 words. The purpose of the theme is to state the main truth or spiritual principle as clearly and as succinctly as possible. Generally there is only one theme to a passage, not many. It may be stated in different ways, but the core should remain the same.

A possible theme for 1 Peter 2 might be stated as follows: "The believer is called to follow the example of the rejected Christ into a life of submission and suffering at the hands of a hostile world."

In a study of the life of Rahab and why she was considered great in God's sight, the theme might be stated as follows: "The reason for Rahab's inclusion in God's Hall of Fame [Hebrews 11] is found in her willingness to take great risks for God on the basis of little knowledge."

Or let us say you are studying the training of the 12 disciples in the years of Jesus' public ministry. What was the *main* thing Jesus sought to impart to them? Your topical study would reveal that the "big idea" Jesus sought to communicate was *faith*. The articulation of your key thought would center around this idea of faith.

If a group was doing a study on what Jesus sought to impart to the disciples, all should conclude that faith was the main truth, though the wording of that truth might vary from person to person.

## Flow

How did the writer get to where he is? How did he arrive at the theme? Determining the flow is the third step in the process of interpretation. It is the movement of the argument, narrative, or teaching. In a topical study the flow is expressed in the natural unfolding of the topic.

Maybe you decide to study the topic of *prayer*. Because it is such a large topic you elect to narrow it to what the Gospel of John teaches about it. The flow is answered in such questions as: "How does John handle the subject of prayer?" "Is it by teaching, example, or combination?" "Through whose life or lives is it seen?"

In another area, you might ask: "How does Jesus go about teaching His disciples faith?" "Is there any pattern?" "Does He combine teaching and experience?"

These three aspects of interpretation, *purpose, key thought,* and *flow* are seen in each of the types of Bible study. It is at the same time both an interesting and an important part of your study. Attack it in a spirit of expectation.

# 10 Correlation: The Role of a Coordinator

**CORRELATION**

**Relating what is being studied with other portions of Scripture and within the section itself.**

One dictionary defines *correlation* as: "To bring two or more things into relation with one another; the act of relating." This is an exciting and highly rewarding aspect of Bible study. In scope it will range from relating one verse to another, to relating one paragraph to another, and to relating the various chapters of a book to one another.

Since the Bible is truth, and all truth due to its divine origin is unified, it is important to relate various truths to one another. It makes the Scriptures coherent and helps the student to be consistent with what the rest of the Bible says on any given subject.

Some basic ways of correlating your study are through cross-references, paraphrases, outlines, and charts.

### Cross-references

This expression of correlation is to compare a word, verse, idea, event, or story with another portion of Scripture. Often the content of one passage will help clarify the content of another. At times you will want to cross-reference the thought with another thought found within the passage you are studying. At other times you will look for the cross-reference outside the passage, but within the book. Then too, there will be times when you will want to go outside the book you are studying into another portion of the Bible.

Several types of cross-references are available for your use.

*Word cross-references*—At times in your study you will discover an important word that you may want to cross reference. It may appear important to the passage and you may want to investigate it further. The person Melchizedek is such an example (Hebrews 5:6). Cross-referencing from within Hebrews, you find him discussed at some length in Chapter 7. Outside of Hebrews, he is introduced in Genesis 14:18 and briefly mentioned in Psalm 110:4.

This kind of cross-reference becomes strategically important in your topical and biographical studies.

*Parallel cross-references*—These are verses or thoughts that say virtually the same thing. Often the wording and context are slightly different, giving you fresh insight on the subject you are studying. The Gospels and some of Paul's epistles are places where this type of cross-reference is readily used. Paul wrote to the Ephesians, "Speak to one another with psalms, hymns, and spiritual songs. Sing and make music in your heart to the Lord" (Ephesians 5:19). You may cross reference that with his exhortation to the Colossians: "Let the word of Christ dwell in you richly as you teach and counsel one another with all wisdom, and as you sing psalms, hymns and spiritual songs with gratitude in your hearts to God" (Colossians 3:16). Comparing the context of these two statements is a fascinating study in and of itself. The parable of the sower in Matthew 13:3-23 may be cross referenced with the parallel accounts in Mark 4:3-20 and Luke 8:4-15.

*Corresponding cross-references*—The New Testament writers frequently quote from the Old Testament. A study of the context of the passage quoted is often helpful in understanding the point the author is making. When Jesus was in Nazareth, the town in which He was raised, He read from the Scroll of Isaiah in the local synagogue (see Luke 4:16-30). When you cross reference Luke 4:18 with Isaiah 61:1-2, you note that Jesus ends His quotation of Isaiah *halfway* through verse 2. Why does He do this? He does this because the Isaiah passage includes both of His comings—the first in humility and the second in glory—and He was at that time in Nazareth only in His first advent.

Another type of corresponding cross-reference is where another portion of Scripture refers to the same event. For example, Paul said, "You know, brothers, that our visit to you was not a failure" (1 Thessalonians 2:1). When did this occur? Luke tells in the Book of Acts (see Acts 17:1-10).

*Idea cross-references*—These are the most helpful cross-references in the analytical study. Here you endeavor to capture the thought of the author in the verse or paragraph being studied and compare it with a similar thought elsewhere in the Bible. The key thought of 1 Peter 1:23, for example, is that a person needs to be born again by the eternal Word of God. When cross referenced with John 3:1-8, you find Jesus saying that a person needs to be born again, but by the Holy Spirit. Why the difference? That is, why does Peter say it is by the Word and Jesus by the Spirit? Because you cannot know the living God apart from the Bible and you cannot know the Bible apart from the Spirit of the living God. The two are inseparable, and for this reason may be interchanged (see also Hebrews 4:12-13).

*Contrasting cross-references*—Contrasting examples in the Bible help you pinpoint proper action as well as bringing into balance a proper understanding of what the Bible teaches on a subject. Perhaps it will be helpful to illustrate both.

Contrast how Jesus handled temptation in Matthew 4 at the beginning of His ministry with how Adam handled it in Genesis 3. The "first Adam" met Satan and was defeated; the "second Adam" met Satan and was victorious.

In Paul's first letter to the Corinthians he makes an interesting comment. "I say this as a concession, not as a command" (1 Corinthians 7:6). Some may conclude that what follows was Paul's idea, and not from the Lord. A contrasting cross-reference brings important balance to this statement. Paul had previously told them, "This is what we speak, not in words taught us by human wisdom but in words taught by the Spirit, expressing spiritual truths in spiritual words" (1 Corinthians 2:13). Here Paul reminds us that even that which is spoken by "concession" is what the Holy Spirit is teaching.

A number of good sources of cross-references are available to you today. If you are cross-referencing a word, use a good concordance such as *Strong's Exhaustive Concordance of the Bible* or *Young's Analytical Concordance to the Bible*. Many Bibles have excellent lists of cross-references in the margins next to the verses or in an abbreviated concordance in the back of the Bible. *The Treasury of Scripture Knowledge* is probably the best source of cross-references. It lists 500,000 difficult cross-references and includes every book in the Bible.

Don't fall into the trap of relying completely on these helps rather than thinking for yourself. Often cross-references that give you the most satisfaction are those you will have thought of yourself.

**Personal Paraphrase**

Another form of correlation is the paraphrase—stating the content of the section you are studying in contemporary language by relating it to itself. Some modern paraphrases provide good examples of this form of correlation. The following excerpts are from *The New Testament in Modern English, Revised Edition* by J. B. Phillips and *The Living Bible* by Kenneth Taylor.

---

**1 Thessalonians 2:7-8 (PH)**

"Our attitude among you was one of tenderness, rather like a nurse caring for her babies. Because we loved you, it was a joy to us to give you not only the Gospel of God but our very hearts—so dear had you become to us."

**1 Thessalonians 2:7-8 (LB)**

"But we were gentle among you as a mother feeding and caring for her own children. We loved you dearly—so dearly that we gave you not only God's message, but our own lives too."

---

Figure 20

**Scripture Versions**

When you are being creative in your personal paraphrasing, do not stray from the basic content of the passage you are studying. Your paraphrase must express the thought of the writer, though in different words.

## Detailed Outline

Some people enjoy using a detailed outline for their correlation of a passage within itself. This type of outline includes every idea mentioned in the section you are studying without omitting any details. Such an outline of 1 Thessalonians 1:1-5 appears in Figure 21.

## I. PAUL'S GREETING (1:1)

A. From: Paul, Silvanus, and Timothy

B. To: The Church of the Thessalonians — in God and Christ

C. Greeting: Grace to you and peace

## II. PAUL'S PRAYER AND GOSPEL MINISTRY (1:2-5)

A. Paul's prayer for the Thessalonians (vv. 2,3)
   1. Always giving thanks for them
   2. Constantly remembering their:
      a. Work of faith ⎫
      b. Labor of love ⎬ in Christ
      c. Steadfastness of hope ⎭ in the presence of God

B. Paul's Gospel Ministry to the Thessalonians (vv. 4-5)
   1. God loved the Thessalonians and chose them
   2. The Gospel came:
      a. In Word
      b. In Power
      c. In the Holy Spirit
      d. With full conviction
   3. Paul's manner of living was for their sake

Figure 21

## Charts

This method of correlation maximizes your opportunity to be creative in your Bible study. For this reason it is for many the most fun and rewarding. The chart is also one of the most effective ways of grasping the unity of a passage, book, or topic. Its purpose is to give you a "bird's eye" view of the principal thoughts, so you can relate them to one another.

The chart is simply one of the many possible tools you may want to use in Bible study. It is not a substitute for your outline or other forms of examination; it can be a helpful augmentation. In fact, your chart will utilize your outline and will be one of the last things you do.

A variety of ways may be used to make a chart. Your selection of the type will depend on what you are trying to accomplish.

## Horizontal Charts

These charts are most helpful in seeing the whole of your study of a passage or book, in comparing various elements in your study, and in making a topical grid. They are versatile, allowing for many possibilities of development and do not follow any rigid rules. Use your creativity and draw them in such a way that they will serve you.

SURVEY CHARTS—These charts enable you to see the whole of your study at one glance, whether it be a passage or a whole book. Take a sheet of paper (8½" x 11" is a good size) and draw a line the long way down the middle. Divide that line according to the number of sections in your study outline. Place your titles (of the outline) in the upper section with the references, and note the correlations in the lower section. Remember, you are trying to relate the parts to the whole visually. Keep the chart neat and orderly, but be creative. You can draw these charts on passages (chapters) and whole books, small or large.

The simplest survey chart is on a chapter, as illustrated in Figure 21. Each section on the chart contains a paragraph and the divisions are indicated by the verse numbers in the corners. Write your paragraph titles at the top of each section, then list the key thoughts that led you to those titles under them; you may want to tie related thoughts together with arrows. Finally, record your con-

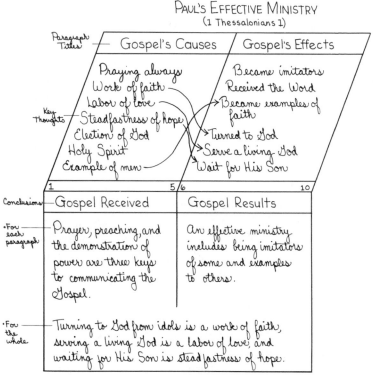

Figure 22

clusions—for each paragraph and for the whole passage—in the
bottom section of the chart. Figure 22 is another variety of a survey
chart on a chapter—1 Thessalonians.

Survey charts of whole books may also vary in complexity.
Figure 23 illustrates a simple chart of 2 Timothy 2; Figure 24 is also
a simple chart; Figure 25 shows more detail on the Book of 1 Peter;
and Figure 26 is a very detailed chart on the Epistle to the Hebrews.

# CALL TO COMMITMENT
## 2 TIMOTHY 2

| | 1 | 7 | 8 | 13 | 14 | 19 | 20 | 26 |
|---|---|---|---|---|---|---|---|---|
| | | FAITHFUL MEN | | FAITHFUL CHRIST | | FAITHFUL WORD | | FAITHFUL SERVANT |
| | | COMMIT | | COMMITMENT | | CONCENTRATE | | CONSECRATE |
| | | TIMOTHY | | PAUL | | | | |
| | | MEN | | MESSAGE | | MINISTRY | | MATURITY |
| | | ENTRUST | | ENDURE | | EQUIP | | EXCELLENCE |
| | | FAITHFULNESS | | | | UNFAITHFULNESS | | |
| | | GRACE | | | | GRACIOUSNESS | | |

HARDSHIP/PERSECUTION SUFFERING — APOSTASY

FAITHFUL MEN INVESTING IN NEEDY PEOPLE

Commitment to a Vision

Commitment to Christ

Commitment to Truth

Commitment to Character

Figure 23

## THE EPISTLE TO THE EPHESIANS

| | PREDETERMINED PURPOSE | PRAYER FOR UNDERSTANDING | PURPOSE APPROPRIATED | PRAYER FOR APPLICATION | PERSONAL RESPONSIBILITIES | PRAYER |
|---|---|---|---|---|---|---|
| | 1:1-14 | 1:15-23 | 2:1 — 3:13 | 3:14-21 | 4:1 — 6:18 | 6:19-20 |
| | DOCTRINE | | | | APPLICATION | |
| | POSITION | | | | RESPONSIBILITY | |
| | PASSIVE | | | | ACTIVE | |
| | WHAT CHRIST DID | | | | WHAT WE DO | |
| | CHURCH'S HEAVENLY POSITION | | | | CHURCH'S EARTHLY CHALLENGE | |
| | INDIVIDUAL | | | | CORPORATE | |
| | GOD'S ACTIONS | | | | OUR PROPOSED REACTIONS | |
| | EXPLANATION OF POSITION | | | | EXHORTATION TO LIVE | |

Figure 24

## 1 PETER
## "SYLLABUS FOR SUFFERING SAINTS"
### "HOW TO HOLD UP, NOT FOLD UP"

GRACE AND PEACE

| SALVATION | SUBMISSION | SUFFERING |
|---|---|---|
| Introduction (1:1-2) Plot Permanent vs. Passing | Introduction (2:11-12) | Conclusion (5:12-14) |
| THE PRIVILEGES OF SALVATION (1:3-12) | IN THE STATE (2:13-17) **CIVIL** | AS A CITIZEN (3:13-4:6) |
| THE PRODUCTS OF SALVATION (1:13-25) | IN THE HOUSEHOLD (2:18-25) **SOCIAL** | AS A SAINT (4:7-19) |
| THE PROCESS OF SALVATION (2:1-10) | IN THE FAMILY (3:1-7) **DOMESTIC** | AS A SHEPHERD (5:1-7) |
| | Summary (3:8-12) | AS A SOLDIER (5:8-11) |
| DOCTRINE IS DYNAMIC! | THE CHRISTIAN'S LIFE-STYLE! | THE CHISEL TO SHAPE THE SOUL! |
| 1:3 ................ 2:10 | 2:11 ................ 3:12 | 3:13 ................ 5:11 |
| THE DESTINY OF THE CHRISTIAN | THE DUTY OF THE CHRISTIAN | THE DISCIPLINE OF THE CHRISTIAN |
| Our Relationship to God | Our Relationship to Others | Our Relationship to Circumstances |
| Our Belief | Our Behavior | Our Buffeting |
| Our Relationship | Our Responsibility | Our Rejoicing |

GRACE AND PEACE

Figure 25

# THE EPISTLE TO THE HEBREWS

## A COMPARISON OF CHRIST TO THE OLD TESTAMENT

### CHRIST: THE FULFILLMENT OF OLD TESTAMENT MESSIANIC PROMISES

**CHRIST THE PERFECT HIGH PRIEST**

HE IS BETTER . . .

| 1:1-14 | 2:1-18 | 3:1-19 | 4:1-16 | 5:1-14 | 6:1-20 | 7:1-28 | 8:1-13 | 9:1—10:18 |
|---|---|---|---|---|---|---|---|---|
| THE PERSON AND WORK OF CHRIST | | THE POSITION OF CHRIST | THE PROVISION OF CHRIST | THE PERFECT PRIESTHOOD OF CHRIST | THE PROMISES OF CHRIST | THE PERFECTION OF CHRIST | THE PLACE OF CHRIST'S MINISTRY | THE PRIESTLY MINISTRY OF CHRIST |
| than Angels | | than Moses | | Rest | than Aaron | Assurance | Priesthood · Covenant | Sacrifice |
| Created the Universe | Redeemed Men | Built the Church | Provided Acceptance | Demonstrated Obedience | Provided a Hope | Intercedes Continuously | Established a Covenant of Grace | Sacrificed Himself |
| | Heed the Word of God 2:1-4 | Don't Be Hardened in Unbelief 3:12-14 | | | Maturity Affects Assurance 5:11—6:12 | | | |

WARNINGS

**CHRIST THE PERFECT WAY**

A BETTER FAITH . . .

| 10:19-39 | 11:1-40 | 12:1-29 | 13:1-25 |
|---|---|---|---|
| ENDURANCE OF FAITH | EXPLANATION AND EXAMPLES OF FAITH | ENCUMBRANCES OF FAITH | EXPRESSIONS OF FAITH |
| Provided a New and Living Way | Gave Promises | Is by Our Side | Is the Same Always |
| Don't Reject Christ 10:26-31 | | Heed the Word of God 12:25-29 | |

| Preeminence of Christ | Preeminence of Christ's Priesthood | Practical Teaching and Exhortation |
|---|---|---|
| What Have We? | We have such a High Priest | Having, therefore, let us . . . |
| INSTRUCTION | | EXHORTATION |
| A NEW COVENANT | | AN OLD FAITH |
| SUPERIOR PERSON | SUPERIOR MINISTRY | SUPERIOR LIFE |
| What Christ Did — His Person | | What We Do — Our Response |

Figure 26

COMPARATIVE CHARTS—These charts are used to sort out a mixture of information for the purpose of comparison and contrast. To make your chart, take a sheet of paper (8½'' x 11'' preferably) and divide it into the desired number of squares. Horizontally state the things to be compared; vertically state the people or events. Figure 28 illustrates this type of chart by comparing the journeys of the Apostle Paul, while Figure 29 charts his imprisonments. (These two charts are not filled in—you can do that sometime— but illustrate the concept.)

A TOPICAL GRID—Many passages of Scripture deal with one particular topic. For example, 1 Corinthians 13 is about love, 1 Corinthians 15 about the resurrection, and 2 Peter 2 about false teachers. The themes of these chapters are usually best stated in a word or phrase, rather than a sentence. Figure 27 illustrates a topical grid on 2 Thessalonians 2.

TOPIC: FOLLOW-UP    CHAPTER: 2 THESSALONIANS 2

| Verse | Positive Characteristics | Negative Attitudes | Relationships | Activities |
|---|---|---|---|---|
| 4 | approved by God; entrusted with Gospel | not speaking to please men | | |
| 5 | | no flattering speech; not greedy. | | |
| 6 | | no glory seeking; not asserting authority | | |
| 7 | gentle | | a nursing mother | caring for them |
| 8 | having fond affection, very dear to them | | | imparting lives |

Figure 27

## PAUL'S JOURNEYS

| Journeys | Scripture | Dates | Places Visited and Length of Stay | Churches Established and the Date | Men Traveling with Paul | Letters Written and Dates |
|---|---|---|---|---|---|---|
| 1 | | | | | | |
| 2 | | | | | | |
| 3 | | | | | | |

Figure 28

## PAUL'S IMPRISONMENTS

| Imprisonments | Scripture | Dates | Men Paul Appeared Before | Reason for Imprisonment | Men Sent out by Paul and Where Sent | Men with Paul | Letters Written and Dates |
|---|---|---|---|---|---|---|---|
| Caesarean | | | | | | | |
| First Roman | | | | | | | |
| Second Roman | | | | | | | |

Figure 29

In the left hand column list the references that will break the chapter up into smaller portions. The smaller portions may be paragraphs, sentences, or individual verses.

Next, determine what you want to investigate about this topic and list these categories horizontally. Some of them are illustrated in Figure 27. This type of chart will correlate the whole chapter for you.

### Vertical Charts

These charts also may be used in different ways: to correlate the content of a chapter or section of a book, to compare and contrast people and events, and to sort out chronological events. Again, you should use your creativity to draw them in such ways that they will be most useful to you.

PASSAGE DESCRIPTION—To correlate the content of a chapter or passage, first divide the chapter you are studying into paragraphs. Mark down the beginning verse and the ending verse of each paragraph on your chart. For example, in 1 Thessalonians 1 you will find two paragraphs, verses 1-5 and verses 6-10.

| 1 THESSALONIANS 1 | |
|---|---|
| | |
| PARAGRAPH 1 — vv. 1-5<br>v. 1 | PARAGRAPH 2 — vv. 6-10<br>v. 6 |
| v. 5 | v. 10 |

Figure 30

The next step is to write in key thoughts from the paragraph in the block allotted to it. Avoid interpretation at this point; just record what you observe.

| 1 THESSALONIANS 1 | |
|---|---|
| | |
| PARAGRAPH 1 — vv. 1-5<br>v. 1 — Paul greets the<br>Thessalonians<br>— Paul prays<br>— Paul brought the<br>Gospel to them<br><br>v. 5 | PARAGRAPH 2 — vv. 6-10<br>v. 6 — The Thessalonians . . .<br>— became imitators<br>— became examples<br>— spread their faith abroad<br>— turned to God<br><br>v. 10 |

Figure 31

The third step is to title your paragraphs. Consider the key thoughts you have written in your chart rather than rereading the biblical text. After you have considered what you wrote for the first paragraph of 1 Thessalonians 1, you might title it, ''The Gospel Received.'' Other possibilities might be ''Paul's Ministry'' or ''The Enlivening Message.''

| 1 THESSALONIANS 1 | |
|---|---|
| **THE GOSPEL RECEIVED** | **THE GOSPEL RESULTS** |
| PARAGRAPH 1 — vv. 1-5<br>v. 1 — Paul greets the<br>Thessalonians<br>— Paul prays<br>— Paul brought the<br>Gospel to them<br><br>v. 5 | PARAGRAPH 2 — vv. 6-10<br>v. 6 — The Thessalonians . . .<br>— became imitators<br>— became examples<br>— spread their faith abroad<br>— turned to God<br><br>v. 10 |

Figure 32

COMPARATIVE CHART—A vertical chart may be used to make comparisons and contrasts. Figure 13 in Chapter 8 is an illustration of this as the ministry of Christ was contrasted with that of Aaron.

CHRONOLOGICAL CHART—This type of chart is particularly helpful in sorting out chronological events in various periods of Bible history. If you, like many, have difficulty following the sequence of events in Israel's history during the period of the divided kingdom, a chart might help you understand those times. After the reign of Solomon (1 Kings 12), Israel was divided into the southern kingdom (Judah) and the northern kingdom (Israel). The division occurred about 931 B.C. The northern kingdom of Israel ended with its deportation at the hands of Assyria in 722 B.C. while Judah ended in 586 B.C. with the Babylonian captivity.

To chart the chronology of this period, place the dates vertically, with 931 at the top of the page, working down through 586 (it may take more than one sheet of paper). Horizontally place the information you want to correlate. Write in the kings of Judah and Israel, the number of years they reigned, their character (whether good or bad), and the active prophet(s) during their reign. Figure 33, a partial chart of the period, includes those elements and shows you how it may be drawn. You may also add other elements, such as, the relationship of each king to his predecessor, how each king died, and the Scripture references. You can add or delete as you want.

## Pyramid Charts

This type of chart is useful in arranging your material to show movement from the specific to the general and vice versa.

Peter opens his first letter with these words: "Praise be to the God and Father of our Lord Jesus Christ! In his great mercy he has given us new birth into a living hope through the resurrection of Jesus Christ from the dead, and into an inheritance that can never perish, spoil or fade—kept in heaven for you" (1 Peter 1:3-4). The progression of his thought is charted in Figure 34.

# PERIOD OF THE DIVIDED KINGDOM

| DATE | JUDAH | | YRS REIGN | GOOD/BAD | ISRAEL | | YRS REIGN | GOOD/BAD | PROPHET |
|---|---|---|---|---|---|---|---|---|---|
| 931 | Rehoboam | 931 | 17 | bad | Jeroboam | 931 | 22 | bad | |
| 925 | | | | | | | | | |
| 920 | | | | | | | | | |
| 915 | Abijam | 913 | 3 | bad | | | | | |
| 910 | Asa | 911 | 41 | good | Nadab | 910 | 2 | bad | |
| 905 | | | | | Baasha | 909 | 24 | bad | |
| 900 | | | | | | | | | |
| 895 | | | | | | | | | |
| 890 | | | | | Elah | 886 | 2 | bad | |
| 885 | | | | | Zimri | 885 | 7 days | bad | |
| 880 | | | | | Omri | 885 | 12 | bad | |
| 875 | Jehoshaphat | 873 | 25 | good | Ahab | 874 | 22 | bad | |
| 870 | | | | | | | | | |
| 865 | | | | | | | | | |
| 860 | | | | | | | | | |
| 855 | Jehoram | 853 | 8 | bad | Ahaziah | 853 | 2 | bad | |
| 850 | | | | | Jehoram | 852 | 12 | bad | |
| 845 | Ahaziah | 841 | 1 | bad | | | | | |
| 840 | Athaliah | 841 | 6 | bad | Jehu | 841 | 28 | bad | |
| 835 | Joash | 835 | 40 | good | | | | | |
| 830 | | | | | | | | | |
| 825 | | | | | | | | | |
| 820 | | | | | | | | | |
| 815 | | | | | Jehoahaz | 814 | 17 | bad | |
| 810 | | | | | | | | | |
| 805 | | | | | | | | | |
| 800 | | | | | | | | | |
| 795 | Amaziah | 796 | 29 | good | Jehoash | 798 | 16 | bad | |

Figure 33

Figure 34

The whole book of 1 Peter has four major themes: sanctification, suffering, salvation, and submission. The Holy Spirit is sanctifying the believer, which builds a contrast between him and the life style of the non-Christian. The unbeliever's reaction is to persecute the Christian. The Christian's response of submission brings about the salvation of the non-Christian. You can chart all that in the manner of Figure 35.

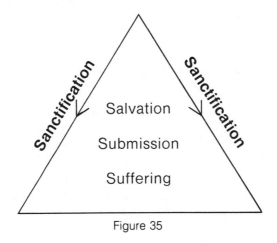

Figure 35

Whenever you have a progression of thought that flows from the general to the specific, this type of chart can be used effectively.

## Illustrative Charts

This method of charting is the most creative of all the methods and also the most difficult to describe or explain. You are familiar with the proverb, "A picture is worth a thousand words." In this type of charting, you seek to draw the truths together in picture form.

Paul pictures God as being sufficient to meet all our needs (Philippians 4:13, 19). One possible way of illustrating this is shown in Figure 36.

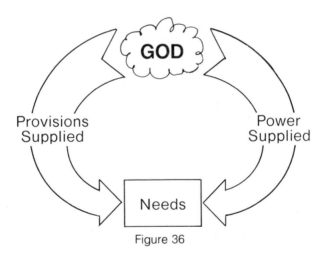

Figure 36

Romans 6–8 details the believer's freedom from the penalty, power, and presence of sin. An example of how this may be charted is found in Figure 37.

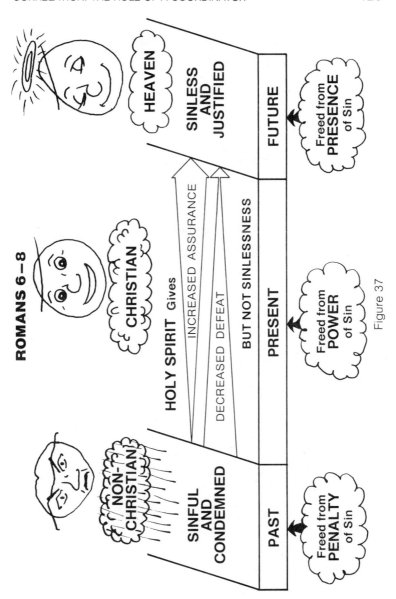

ROMANS 6–8

NON-CHRISTIAN

SINFUL AND CONDEMNED

CHRISTIAN

HOLY SPIRIT Gives

INCREASED ASSURANCE

DECREASED DEFEAT

BUT NOT SINLESSNESS

HEAVEN

SINLESS AND JUSTIFIED

PAST

PRESENT

FUTURE

Freed from PENALTY of Sin

Freed from POWER of Sin

Freed from PRESENCE of Sin

Figure 37

You can incorporate many creative approaches into your study as long as you include the content of the passage under study. Two examples of illustrative charts from 1 Thessalonians 1 are shown in Figures 38 and 39.

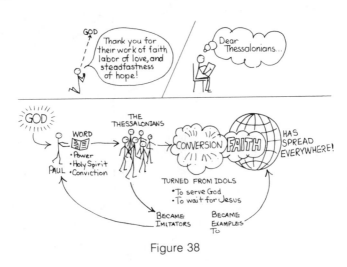

Figure 38

Figure 39

## *Combination Charts*

At times you will want to combine the various methods of charting. Figure 40 is a chart giving an overview of Hebrews 7. It combines the *horizontal* and *illustrative* methods. Another is shown in Figure 41, in which the *horizontal* and *vertical* elements are combined.

## Summary

The need to be creative in this aspect of Bible study cannot be overemphasized. So experiment. Try all kinds of things, combining what you have learned here with some of your own ideas. Use colored pens for contrast and keeping track of the movement of your ideas. Remember, your objective is to correlate the various truths in your study to one another, and in so relating them to discover new truth. Don't be intimidated by the newness of the approach or the variety of methods. Start with a portion you can handle, and go from there.

Let your creative instincts take over. Remember, the methodology is to help *you* get a grasp on the passage under study.

**THE PERFECTION OF CHRIST**
HIS IS A BETTER PRIESTHOOD
Hebrews 7:1-28

| HIS PERSON | | HIS PROMISE | | HIS PERFORMANCE | |
|---|---|---|---|---|---|
| Credentials of Melchizedek | Consideration of His Greatness | Change Needed in the Old Order | Covenant Established by an Oath | Contrasting Abilities in the Priesthoods | Christ's Sacrifice of Himself |
| 7:1-3 | 7:4-10 | 7:11-19 | 7:20-22 | 7:23-25 | 7:26-28 |
| BETTER ORDER | | BETTER COVENANT | | BETTER PRIEST | |
| WHO HE WAS | | WHY HE CAME | | WHAT HE DID | |
| BECAUSE HE IS FROM MELCHIZEDEK | | HE IS NOT LIMITED BY SINAI | | HE IS NOT LIMITED BY THE ALTAR | |

Figure 40

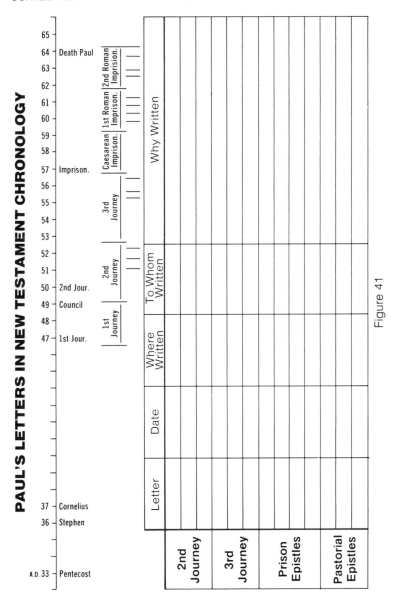

PAUL'S LETTERS IN NEW TESTAMENT CHRONOLOGY

Figure 41

# Application: The Role of an Implementor

**APPLICATION**

Implementing what has been studied to daily Christian living.

Throughout the centuries, the application of God's Word constantly expresses itself as *the* major need in Christianity. Even in Bible times God again and again rebuked His people for failure to make application of His truths. James put it this way: "Do not merely listen to the Word, and so deceive yourselves. Do what it says" (James 1:22).

Learning is far easier than applying. If you find this to be true in your own life, you are no different than most Christians. Yet God

131

insists on your working at applying His truths to your life.

Rule Six under the principles of interpretation states, "The primary purpose of the Bible is to change our lives, not increase our knowledge." In this part of your Bible study program you are prayerfully endeavoring to bring your life more completely into conformity with God's standards.

In making a personal application it is important to distinguish between emotion and volition. Often applying God's Word is an emotional experience. However, *action* and not just feeling is what God wants. Jesus' parable of the two sons makes this point quite clear (see Matthew 21:28-32). The father asked the first son to work in the vineyard, but he refused to go. Later he changed his mind and obeyed his father. The second son readily agreed to go when asked, but never showed up for work. "Which of the two did what his father wanted?" was the question Jesus asked (Matthew 21:31). You would agree that it was the first. Ideally the Lord wants both your emotions and volition, but it is when you *do* what God wants that you make application.

## Procedure for Making Applications

The following seven steps are a helpful mechanical procedure for making applications.

1. *Use the Principle of Observation*. Include in your observation section of Bible study "possible" points of application as you discover them. (These have been illustrated in each of the observation sections of the five methods of Bible study.) Mark them with a colored pen or put (**A**) in the margin so you can identify them. List as many possible applications as you can, for you will find that every passage is "loaded" with them. Ask the Holy Spirit to help you dig them out. InterVarsity Press, in their little booklet titled *Quiet Time*, offers six suggestions—all in the form of questions—that are helpful in stimulating your mind as to possible applications. They are:

- Is there any example for me to follow?
- Is there any command for me to obey?
- Is there any error for me to avoid?
- Is there any sin for me to forsake?
- Is there any promise for me to claim?
- Is there any new thought about God Himself?

2. *Follow the Rules of Interpretation.* A proper application can only be made after you have correctly interpreted the passage. This principle is elaborated on in Rule Six, Corollary 2 in the first book of this trilogy, *A Layman's Guide to Interpreting the Bible.* There may be many applications of a passage, but only one correct interpretation.

Remember too, a literal interpretation is always best unless the text demands otherwise. Rule Ten in *Layman's Guide to Interpreting the Bible* may be reviewed for an elaboration of this point.

3. *Be Selective.* Prayerfully review the possible applications you have listed in the observation section of your study. Select the one you feel the Holy Spirit would have you work on now. Don't try to choose more than one as this can prove to be counterproductive. If you try to apply too many, you will become frustrated and unable to apply any. It is like someone throwing a dozen eggs to you. Trying to catch them all can cause you to miss them all. Select one, make sure you catch it, and let the rest go by.

The process is subjective simply because it is between you and the Lord. If your heart is open and teachable, He will reveal what He wants you to apply.

4. *Be Specific.* Resist the temptation to address yourself to generalities. Put your finger on the heart of the problem and press.

For example, "Philippians 2:5—'God would have me to be more like Jesus'" is too general.

On the other hand, the following is a more specific way of making an application. "When Paul said that Jesus took on Himself 'the very nature of a servant' (Philippians 2:7), I realized that I have not been serving my family as I should. I sit around and let my wife and children wait on me and find myself resenting it when I have to go out of my way to do anything for them.''

5. *Be Personal*. How easy it is to use pronouns such as ''we,'' ''us,'' ''they,'' and ''our'' when making application. How hard it is to talk in terms of ''I,'' ''me,'' ''my,'' and ''mine.'' This is not ''our'' problem; it is ''my'' problem. When writing your applications, stick to the first person singular pronouns.

6. *Write Out Your Application*. As an integral and essential part of your study, the application should be written out. It is hard on pride to verbalize on paper areas of personal application, but you will find it extremely helpful in your quest to do business with God. Writing it out affords an opportunity to go back and check your progress against what you specifically vowed before God you would do.

7. *Set Up a Check-up Procedure*. Sometimes your application will require one specific thing like returning a book you borrowed months before, or apologizing to someone for a wrong you did. At other times your application will require time. It may be a habit God wants you to break, or a series of steps you may have to take like paying installments on a large overdue bill. Then too there will be times when the Holy Spirit will give you a long-range project to work on such as working on an attitude or a virtue.

For example, you are studying the life of Moses and note as a possible application Numbers 12:3, ''Now the man Moses was very *meek*, above all the men which were upon the face of the earth.'' You look up the word *meek* to obtain a precise definition and find it means, ''Enduring injury with patience and without resentment'' *(Webster's)*. The Holy Spirit speaks to you about your unwillingness to let people take advantage of you without a fight. You list specific illustrations when this has been true in your life, but you also realize that a proper application is going to take a major re-working of your attitude.

This type of an application may require a year to work on—not to the exclusion of any further applications during the year—but certainly as the major area on which you will be working. Numerous short-range applications may need to be made throughout the year, but this is the major long-range one.

The longer an application takes, the more difficult it is to check up on the progress. Also, applications dealing with attitudes and motives are harder to measure than those dealing with specific points of action. All of this must be taken into consideration when seeking ways to check up on yourself.

Returning to the application of meekness taken from the life of Moses, a possible plan of attack would be:

- "I will memorize Numbers 12:3 and review it daily throughout the year."
- "I will write *meek* on a card and tape it to the mirror in the bathroom, so that daily I will be reminded of my need to work on this. Each morning I will review Numbers 12:3 and pray about its application in my life for *that* day."
- "I will share this need with my spouse and with [a friend], who knows me well. Once a month I will talk over my progress with them and ask for a frank evaluation."

### Example of a Typical Application

Following is an example of an application that might be written from a study of Philippians 3.

*The passage*—"In my study of Philippians 3 the Holy Spirit convicted me of my gluttony through verses 18-19: 'For, as I have often told you before and now say again even with tears, many live as enemies of the cross of Christ. Their destiny is destruction, their god is their stomach, and their glory is in their shame. Their mind is on earthly things.'"

*An example*—"The other day we were over to the home of Mrs. Jones for dinner and she had prepared the most delicious fried chicken I had ever seen. I overate totally. I knew at the time I was doing it, and felt uncomfortable and embarrassed afterward. I simply love good food.''

*The solution*—''I must 'put a knife to my throat.' When I eat, especially in the home of another, I will take but *one* helping and a moderate one at that.''

*The specific steps*—''To insure that I follow through on this application, I covenant before God that I will:

''1. During grace before each meal, silently ask the Lord to enable me to eat moderately.

''2. Ask my spouse to kick me under the table each time I become immoderate as a gentle reminder of my vow before God.

''3. Write a note of apology to Mrs. Jones for the way I behaved at her table. This will be hard, but it will reinforce my determination never to do it again.''

## Summary

By its very nature, an application is a personal thing. The above are suggestions on how you can put "shoe leather" on your desire to apply the Scriptures. The next book in this trilogy, *A Layman's Guide to Applying the Bible*, gives more practical helps. The bottom line, however, is a change in your character. This change must originate from within. The Holy Spirit will give you wisdom and the courage of your convictions as you apply His Word.

# Appendix

**LONG RANGE STUDY PROGRAM**

**Two plans: 7 years and 10 years**

This suggested program is arranged for 45 weeks of study each year. A two-week synthetic study is scheduled for each book of the Bible—an introductory survey study before and a concluding summary study after. (This means that seven weeks are allowed for a five-chapter book like 1 Thessalonians.). *Topical* and *Biographical* studies are *italicized*. The order of topical studies assumes a person has already been fairly well grounded in basic doctrines through question-and-answer studies. Old Testament chapter studies are underlined.

This program is not meant to be a rigid one, and you may adjust it as you feel you need for your own study program. Interchange books, topics, biographies, and Old Testament chapters, adding or deleting as you think best.

| **First Year** | **Weeks** |
|---|---|
| 1 Thessalonians | 7 |
| 1 John | 7 |
| Philippians | 6 |
| *Salvation* | 2 |
| *Witnessing* | 2 |
| *Follow-up* | 2 |
| Gospel of Mark | 18 |
| *Biographical: Daniel* (Daniel 1–6) | 1 |

## Second Year                                              **Weeks**

Colossians                                                      6
*Jesus Christ* (deity, death, resurrection)                     3
1 Timothy                                                       8
*Biographical: Timothy* (use a concordance)                     1
Gospel of John                                                 23
*Prayer*                                                        2
*Biographical: Josiah* (2 Kings 22–23;
      2 Chronicles 34–35)          1
Isaiah 52:13–53:12                                              1

## Third Year

Galatians                                                       8
*The Holy Spirit and the Lordship of Christ*                    3
Ephesians                                                       8
*Biographical: Barnabas* (use a
      concordance)                 1
Romans                                                         18
Exodus 20                                                       1
2 Timothy                                                       6

## Fourth Year

*The Word of God*                                               2
Titus                                                           5
*Biographical: Gideon* (Judges 6–8)                             1
*Obedience*                                                     1
*Biographical: Joseph* (Genesis 28–50)                          2
Acts                                                           30
Exodus 12                                                       1
*Pacesetting*                                                   1
Genesis 3                                                       1
*World Vision*                                                  1

| **Fifth Year** | **Weeks** |
|---|---|
| 1 Peter | 7 |
| *Suffering* | 1 |
| <u>Joshua 1</u> | 1 |
| 1 Corinthians | 18 |
| *Biographical: Elijah* (1 Kings 17–22; 2 Kings 1–2) | 1 |
| *The Will of God* | 2 |
| Hebrews | 15 |

| **Sixth Year** | |
|---|---|
| 2 Thessalonians | 5 |
| *Stewardship and Generosity* | 2 |
| <u>Genesis 22</u> | 1 |
| *Love* | 2 |
| <u>Psalm 1</u> | 1 |
| *The Second Coming of Christ* | 3 |
| <u>Psalm 2</u> | 1 |
| *Biographical: Hezekiah* (2 Kings 18–20; 2 Chronicles 29–32; Isaiah 35–39) | 2 |
| Gospel of Luke | 26 |
| *The Church, Church Growth, and Other Christian Works* | 2 |

| **Seventh Year** | |
|---|---|
| James | 7 |
| *The Tongue* | 1 |
| *Temptation and Victory* | 1 |
| *Purity* | 1 |
| *Biographical: Elisha* (2 Kings 1–13) | 1 |
| 2 Peter | 5 |
| *Repentance* | 1 |
| *Sin* | 2 |

|                                               | **Weeks** |
|-----------------------------------------------|:---------:|
| *Satan*                                       | 2         |
| Psalm 23                                      | 1         |
| Psalm 37                                      | 1         |
| 2 Corinthians                                 | 15        |
| 1 Samuel 17                                   | 1         |
| 2 Samuel 7                                    | 1         |
| *Discipline and Diligence*                    | 1         |
| *Good Works*                                  | 1         |
| Proverbs 2                                    | 1         |
| Psalm 78                                      | 1         |
| 2 John                                        | 1         |

## Seven-year Summary:

| 23 New Testament Books (Mark through 2 John) | 249 |
|----------------------------------------------|:---:|
| 24 *Topical Studies*                         | 41  |
| 9 *Biographical Studies*                     | 11  |
| 14 Old Testament Chapters                    | 14  |
| Seven Years at 45 Weeks per Year             | 315 |

## Eighth Year

| 3 John                                      | 1  |
|---------------------------------------------|:--:|
| Jude                                        | 1  |
| *Humility*                                  | 1  |
| *Honesty*                                   | 1  |
| Revelation                                  | 24 |
| *Judgment and Hell*                         | 2  |
| *Biographical: Nehemiah* (Nehemiah 1–13)    | 2  |
| Genesis 1                                   | 1  |

| | Weeks |
|---|---|
| Genesis 12 | 1 |
| Philemon | 1 |
| *Redeeming the Time* | 1 |
| *Biographical: Peter* (use a concordance) | 5 |
| Judges 7 | 1 |
| 1 Kings 18 | 1 |
| Job 1 | 1 |
| Job 2 | 1 |

## Ninth Year

| | |
|---|---|
| Gospel of Matthew | 30 |
| *Correction and Rebuke* | 1 |
| 2 Kings 17 | 1 |
| Psalm 40 | 1 |
| Numbers 14 | 1 |
| *Faithfulness—God's; Man's Required* | 2 |
| Psalm 103 | 1 |
| Deuteronomy 4 | 1 |
| Joshua 3 | 1 |
| Jonah | 6 |

In the Tenth Year you may begin again, selecting from the previous nine, or you may add any other Old Testament books, topics, and biographies that you desire.